A *Christian's*
View of the Torah

Matt P. Simmons

WestBow
PRESS
A DIVISION OF THOMAS NELSON

Copyright © 2012 by Matt P. Simmons

All rights reserved. No part of this book may be used or reproduced by any means, graphic, electronic, or mechanical, including photocopying, recording, taping or by any information storage retrieval system without the written permission of the publisher except in the case of brief quotations embodied in critical articles and reviews.

Scripture quotations, unless otherwise noted, quoted scripture is from The Holy Bible, New International Version, Copyright 1984, International Bible Society.

WestBow Press books may be ordered through booksellers or by contacting:

WestBow Press
A Division of Thomas Nelson
1663 Liberty Drive
Bloomington, IN 47403
www.westbowpress.com
1-(866) 928-1240

Because of the dynamic nature of the Internet, any web addresses or links contained in this book may have changed since publication and may no longer be valid. The views expressed in this work are solely those of the author and do not necessarily reflect the views of the publisher, and the publisher hereby disclaims any responsibility for them.

Any people depicted in stock imagery provided by Thinkstock are models, and such images are being used for illustrative purposes only.

Certain stock imagery © Thinkstock.

Library of Congress Control Number: 2011963394

ISBN: 978-1-4497-3545-6 (sc)
ISBN: 978-1-4497-3544-9 (e)

Printed in the United States of America

WestBow Press rev. date: 3/13/2012

Table of Contents

A Note from the Author	vii
Prologue	ix
1. Why Six Days?	1
2. Fall from Perfection	7
3. Forty!	11
4. Themes on Abram	15
5. Why Was Ishmael Born?	19
6. Circumcision	23
7. What Could Have Saved Sodom and Gomorrah?	27
8. Isaac on the Altar	31
9. Meeting Your Bride at the Well	35
10. Joseph and Judah	39
11. The Jewish Iliad	43
12. I AM!	47
13. God's War	55
14. Why Is This Night Different?	59
15. The First Harvest	63
16. The Tabernacle	67
17. The Priest	73
18. Sacrifices	77
19. Elements of Worship	81
20. The Feasts	85
21. Temptations	89
22. Balaam	95
23. It is Finished	101
Bibliography	107
Other Readings	109

A Note from the Author

My experience has been that most books of biblical study fall into two extremes. One, the books are a guide for the uninitiated or new Christian and are so simplistic that they give no new insights to a Christian wanting to grow. Two, the other extreme, they are so theological that you need a doctorate in divinity to get anything out of them. Few strive to touch the middle ground, which allows the average Christian to grow and to add to his faith.

This book is an attempt to fill that middle-ground need. It is not intended as an evangelistic tool but as an aid for those who wish to move from the milk to the meat of the Word. As such, I am suggesting that the reader have a good working knowledge of the Bible. You should have read the entire Bible at least once and have a good knowledge of the Torah, Historical Books, the Gospels, Acts, and the Epistles. (In short, Genesis through Second Chronicles and Matthew through Jude.)

I must warn the reader that I'm not a theologian or a Biblical scholar in the traditional sense. My background is in science and technology, specifically mathematics and engineering. I'm sure many learned people will find weaknesses (if not out right errors) in some of my points, but my goal is to help fellow Christians grow by stimulating their thinking. With that in mind, take everything I say with a very large grain of salt. Feel free to disagree with me. But when you do, make sure you disagree for scriptural reasons and not because the idea is unfamiliar.

Prologue

What is the Bible? A simple question, but the answer is critical.

Some will give the simple answer: the Word of God. But that begs the question. Science and nature are also divine outpourings and can be seen as the Word of God. So what specifically is the Bible: history, allegory, or myth? Responding to that question determines how we study scripture and colors our understanding.

The Bible can be seen as a purely teaching instrument and, therefore, a "collection of allegories and parables." It is also viewed as a collection of myths and legends. This view is usually held among nonbelievers, but an ever-growing body of professed believers is donning those views. The Bible has been studied from the scientific, or the historical and archeological, point of view. This method is usually used by those who want to "prove" the Bible. All of the methods have their strengths and weaknesses. To be honest, the weaknesses outnumber the strengths. If the Bible is viewed as a myth or fable, then it lacks divine authority and can be ignored when inconvenient. In such cases, it has no anchor in absolute truth; it becomes a victim of temporal morals and fashion. If studied solely from the factual disciplines, then it's a hostage of current understanding. If such understanding ever appears to conflict with the Bible, then faith will suffer because its foundation was placed on the shifting sands of man's limited and temporal understanding of science or history. (This in not to say there is any conflict between scripture or science and history. All seeming conflict is in the human mind. Perfect understanding of scripture, history and science would have perfect harmony. And that is an article of faith.)

There is one method of exploration that is rarely used: to view the Bible as a work of art, particularly literature. In many ways, this method makes the most sense. After all, God is the fountainhead of all art and is Himself the greatest artist of all. Being our creator, He knows which techniques will have the greatest impact on our minds, emotions and souls.

Moreover, where a human artist must choose to work in weak and limited media—paint, clay, ink, or sound—the Lord works in the far more awesome medium of history! Humanity is in the unique position of being both the artwork and the audience.

With this method, the Bible is viewed holistically, with parallels, symbols and themes constantly repeated and emphasized. God uses both history and scripture to present Himself to humanity, to explain our place in creation, and to show our duty to God

It shouldn't be all that surprising to see the Bible interconnected with all the stories pointing to one thing. After all, God is all-powerful. He is the one who sets the stage for the drama to unfold. He is the one who caused a family to flee from one place just so 100 years later a boy can be born at the right place to affect history. God allows a disaster to cause one story to be lost while another survives. He makes the memory to fail in some facts and be more vivid for others. All of this transpires over the millennia so that the Bible can come to express God's true intent.

If God is all-powerful and if the Bible is His word, then every passage has a purpose and a meaning. The reader must constantly ask why. Why is this story so prominent? Why did God permit this action to happen? When a reasonable answer is found, then true insight is obtained.

1

Why Six Days?

When studying chapter 1 of Genesis, you must realize that giving a time for creation is not the main thrust. In fact, the time of the world's beginning is completely irrelevant. Whether the days were actually twenty-four hours, or not, has no bearing on anything in faith. What is vital is to ask this, why did God place the first chapter of Genesis in the Bible at all?

Because God is all-powerful, He could have created the universe in a nanosecond. If He had done so, then the narrative could have started at the second chapter. However, because the first chapter is there, this question must be asked, why six days for creation and a seventh to rest? There are three very good explanations.

There is a Hebrew literary convention called chiasmus by theologians. Chiasmus is derived form the Greek letter *chi*, which resembles the modern day "X." In this method, each passage has a reflective passage around a core passage that forms an "X."[1] The creation story could be a Hebrew chiasmus. Consider how it is laid out day by day:

Day one—light, with day and night.
  Day two—expanse of water above and below.
    Day three—dry land among the seas and plants.
      Day four—sun, moon, and stars.
    Day five—fish and birds.
  Day six—beasts of the field and man.
Day seven—Sabbath or rest.

It's interesting that the sun and moon are in the center of creation. This placement is not to suggest that the Bible is espousing a heliocentric system before Copernicus. To suggest so is to place things in scripture that don't exist. However, it does suggest that the Earth—and humanity—were never the center of creation. It was man's feeling of self-importance through Greek philosophy that placed him, and the world, in the center. Man has to stop his navel gazing and realize that he is not the center of the physical universe nor is he the center of the spiritual realm.

The second answer could rest in the very numbers themselves. People must realize that, because Abraham came from Ur of the Chaldeans, the Bible is rooted in Sumerian culture. The Chaldeans and Babylonians saw a certain mystic value in numbers, which held universal truths. (Some of this mysticism was passed throughout the Middle East and Mediterranean area, eventually coming to us through the Greeks.)

Odd numbers were seen as masculine since they could not be evenly divided, and except for the number two, all prime numbers are odd. Likewise, even numbers were viewed as weak; therefore, they were feminine. "One," then, represented male and "two" represented female. Even the ancient numeric symbols of a single line for one and dual lines for two are reminiscent of male and female genitalia.

The number three is, of course, the number for marriage and family with the joining of male and female. But three was also the number for deity. Christians surely think of the Trinity, but the symbolism goes much deeper. God embodies both the masculine and the feminine. He seeks justice and mercy; He sits in judgment and nurtures. The statement "making man in Our image" has a special meaning in this light. It shows that the complete man is the union of male and female.

Also, in ancient Chaldean numerology, the number nine was seen as especially divine. Just like the Jewish Gematria, number values were assigned to different letters (or aspects), except nine was not used. The number was so sacred that they refused to use it in the mundane task of guiding mortals in their daily affairs. This decision is understandable because nine is the combination of three threes.

The number four symbolizes creation. This is seen in the four seasons marked by the winter solstice, vernal equinox, the summer solstice, and the autumnal equinox. As well as the four cardinal points: north, east, south, and west. And it's emphasized in the ancient view of the world being made of four elements: earth, wind, water, and fire. Modern physics still has the number four tied to the universe. But instead of the four elements, we have the four forces: gravity, electromagnetic, strong atomic, and weak atomic.

With the number three for God and number four for creation, it is easy to understand why the numbers seven and twelve are so prominent in the Bible. Seven, which is the adding of three and four, symbolizes God in harmony with His creation. Furthermore, twelve, which is the multiplication of three and four, demonstrates God's glory through His handiwork. Why else choose twelve signs of the Zodiac or twelve inches to a foot. Even the choice of twelve months to the year is somewhat forced. With a twenty-eight day orbit, the moon completes thirteen cycles in a year. True, the Earth's orbit of the sun extends the lunar phases slightly beyond the orbit frequency but not to the extent of the extra days added on the calendar. Finally, isn't it curious that the day was broken into two twelve-hour periods of day and night?

Which leads to this question, why six days? There is a particular class of numbers called perfect numbers.[2] Perfect numbers are ones that when all their divisors, except for the number itself, are added together the sum equals the number. One such number is twenty-eight. Twenty-eight can be broken into two sets of fourteen, four sets of seven, or twenty-eight sets of one. Add those values together (1 + 2 + 4 + 7 + 14), and the sum is twenty-eight. To the ancients, this showed an additional perfection in the universe with twenty-eight days in the lunar orbit. Moreover, perfection existed in the cycle of life with the average menstrual cycle of twenty-eight days. The next perfect number is 496, but the first perfect number is six (1 + 2 + 3).

The number of days is the message, not the length of time. By taking six days to make the world, God saying that what He made was perfect. By resting on the seventh day, He showed the world to be in perfect harmony with Him.

The unfortunate thing is that man can now look at this world and see it is far from perfect. That is the point of the remaining story of the Garden of Eden. It explains why a world so perfect in creation is so imperfect now and why mankind requires redemption.

There is one last thing to notice in the days of creation. It is something that is often found in great literature: the use of symbols, parallelisms, and reflections. The keys are what happened on the first, sixth, and seventh days. They are especially wondrous from the Christian perspective.

First, let's look at the sixth day. The main occurrence was the creation of Adam—the coming to life of one who the Gospel of Luke[3] refers to as a "Son of God." Paul explains that, through one man, death and sin were ushered into the world.[4] He further points out that through one man, life and redemption were returned to the world, another Son of God. From one son, death resulted from his birth; from the other son, life came from His death.

On the seventh day, God took a harmonious rest to reflect on His creation. Our Lord rested in His tomb on another seventh day.

The first day God created light for the physical world. On another first day, a light was resurrected in the spiritual world. As John said, the Word is the light of the world,[5] and in Genesis, God "spoke" and there was light.

From the very story of creation, God was pointing to what would be. He knew of man's need for redemption before the world was created, and He knew what the cost of that redemption would be. Yet He still chose to create.

Who's Perspective?

My professional life has been tied to science and technology, and like many people in that area, I have struggled with the creation story in Genesis. I accept that it is true, but I also accept that what science has discovered is equally true. So how do I reconcile that both are true but seem to contradict. I have found a way to reconcile science and faith, and maybe I can help others who struggle with this seeming contradiction.

A physicist gave me this little problem. Two spaceships are traveling along the same vector. One is trailing the other, and both are going the speed of light. Now there are three possibilities: (a) the leading ship will widen the distance between the two ships, (b) the trailing ship will close the gap between them, or (c) the distance between the two stays the same. Which answer is correct? They all are. It all depends on which perspective (or frame of reference) you examine the problem. If you work the math from the leading ship, it is out running the trailing ship. But to the trailing ship the gab is closing. From outside both ships, the distance between them never changes.

So now think about it, from whose perspective is Genesis chapter 1 being told? Whose frame of reference is the only one in existence at that time? Obviously, it's God's. Remember, God is not in the universe. He exists outside of what we call the space-time continuum. For Him, all of time, all of the universe, all of existence, and all of history are laid out in front of Him like a painting is laid out in front of us. To God, everything from beginning to end—and all that's in between—happened in one instance. What seems to us as a change of order is actually a change of emphasis—God sees everything as the same. Our limited minds force an order and a length of time. We must remember that with the Lord "one day is like a thousand years, and a thousand years are like one day."[6] What we read into scripture as instantaneous could have been thousands or millions of years. For example, we assume that God made man and within seconds gave him a soul, but the time between the two could have been hundreds of thousands of years. It all depends on the perspective.

Chapter 1 Endnotes

[1] John Dart, "Scriptural Schemes: The ABCBAs of Biblical Writing," *Christian Century*, July 13, 2004.
[2] Stanley Gudder, *A Mathematical Journey*, 144–51 (New York: McGraw-Hill, 1994).
[3] Luke 3:23–37.
[4] Romans 5:12–19.
[5] John 1:1–10.
[6] II Peter 3:8.

2

Fall from Perfection

What is the essence of a soul? Is it intellect? Is "I think therefore I am" the foundation of the soul? But an infant is a living soul who has no intellect. Conversely, the serpent of Eden was an intellect without a soul.

Scripture says that the serpent is the craftiest of creatures, but the word crafty should be viewed in the archaic meaning. The modern word would be discerning or perceptive. Most, if not everything, that the serpent told Eve was true. When Eve ate the fruit, she did not die—at least not immediately and not bodily. And God declared, "The man has now become like one of us, knowing good and evil."[1] Surely everything the serpent said was true, but the truth wasn't everything the serpent said. Sometimes the greater lie is holding back some of the truth. The serpent deceived Eve by not telling her that the new knowledge would separate her from God. Her lost innocence would never be regained, and all souls would be twisted and perverted by her actions. If the serpent had told the whole truth, Eve might never have eaten the fruit.

Pity Eve for her deception, but also scorn her for her tragic mistake. She made the mistake that many self-righteous people make. She made her own addition to God's commandment, and then she convinced herself that her addition was God's commandment. Eve added the clause "must not touch,"[2] while God said only "must not eat."[3] It might have been prudent for her to flee temptation by not touching, but it is always dangerous to confuse man's constraint with God's command. Rabbinical tradition has the serpent pushing Eve against the tree before saying, "You will not surely die."[4] Once her constraint was shown to be false, it wasn't much of a leap to mistakenly assume God's command was false. That error is the same one sinners have been making ever since.

In many ways, Adam is the most tragic and the most despicable character of this story. Ancient and medieval theologians blame humanity's fall on Eve, but she was deceived. Her deception can be excused. Where is Adam's excuse? He ate the fruit for no other reason than his rebellious desire to be as God. Who has the greatest fault, the one deceived into sin or the one entering into sin with his eyes wide open?

Those three characters of the Fall give us some insight of what exactly is a soul. Once man lost his innocence, he was divorced from the divine, and his desire has always been to return to it. Man is the only creature that builds an altar and lays a sacrifice on it. And it is true for all men. Many have tried to remove God, but all they have done is replace Him. Some replace Him with philosophical truth, others with scientific knowledge, and some with the idea of the proletariat state. The essence of a soul is man's need to be part of something higher than himself. In short, man's desire to connect with the divine is his soul, and we see this desire particularly in the story of the generation that follows.

Both Cain and Able sought God, but each in a different way. And those two varying ways are how man still seeks God to this day. Both offered sacrifices from the fruits of their labor, but Cain's was rejected while Abel's was accepted. Why? Scripture is silent of any command from God about the particulars of sacrifice or of Him even asking for a sacrifice. The sacrifices seem to be a natural expression of their desire for God. So why was one accepted and one rejected?

Genesis gives some insight to why "Abel offered God a better sacrifice."[5] Geneses 4:3 says that Cain brought "some" of the fruits of the soil, while verse 4 states that Abel brought the "first born" of his flock. Abel showed his faith in God's provision, while Cain gave whatever excess he had. The difference is acknowledging all abundance comes from God, including the abundance of righteousness.

By placing God first, Abel acknowledged his own sinfulness and asked God to forgive. Cain, however, displayed his thankfulness to God for the blessing of the harvest, but, at the same time, claimed sinlessness. He in effect told God that because he had not been deceived and ate the fruit, he was sinless and, therefore, had his own righteousness. God always rejects the self-righteous.

Later, when God says, "sin is crouching at your door; it desires to have you, but you must mater it."[6] God is telling Cain to recognize what is in him. If he fails to come to God, then evil will overwhelm Cain, and he will truly be sinful.

Unfortunately, Cain didn't listen to God. He had the typical reaction of the self-righteous when put to shame by the truly righteous. Rather than accepting his own sin, he instead sought to destroy the righteous one.

Abel was the first righteous man to be killed for putting the self-righteous to shame. He was a sign that pointed to another that was to come—the ultimate righteous man but to death. But Abel isn't a parallel; he's a reflection. Both his and Christ's blood calls out to God. In Abel's case, his blood called for justice to be brought on the evil sinner, while the Messiah's blood called—and is still calling—for mercy on the unrighteous.[7]

So shows the two sides of God in constant conflict: the yang of justice and the yen for mercy. This duality is shown in the Garden of Eden, for in its center stood the tree of the knowledge of good and evil and the tree of life. Knowledge, especially of good and evil, is required for justice. And life is the result of mercy. Those conflicting needs of God, to be just and merciful, are harmonized in only one thing—the blood of Christ.

Chapter 2 Endnotes

[1] Genesis 3:22.
[2] Genesis 3:3.
[3] Genesis 2:17.
[4] Genesis 3:4.
[5] Hebrews 11:4.
[6] Genesis 4:7.
[7] Hebrews 12:24.

3
Forty!

The story of the flood is, in many ways, the most unusual in that it is the least unique. Almost every culture has some story of a catastrophic flood that wipes out all life and often destroys an advanced civilization. This story is found in Sumerian, Greek, Egyptian, and even Native American mythology. It's as if a prehistoric echo is resonating in humanity's collective memory

The story is instructive to the Christian from many points. In Peter's first letter he showed it to be a precursor to baptism.[1] An elect few were saved by water and their faith from a sinful world. The parallels are stark and easily seen. It can, and in many ways should, be viewed as an allegory of every journey through life made by the faithful.

Like Noah, everyone is alone in a sinful world. Everyone must build his own ark of faith to find salvation from God's justifiable vengeance on a sinful world. This story is the first of many where God spares the righteous few from His vengeance on the wicked many. This story, along with Sodom and Gomorrah, as well as the tenth plague of Egypt, points to God's gracious salvation to the faithful few.

There is another facet of the story that should not be lost—that mystical number forty, so prominent in scripture, first appears here. It forces the question, why is forty so important?

Chapter 1 gave a short review of many of the numbers the ancients held as having mystical significance. The number forty doesn't really fit with them. It is not a combination of three, four, six, seven, or twelve. The closest is the combination of four and ten, as in a mixture of creation and completeness. But why should such a mixture be seen as important?

Perhaps with a quick survey of scripture and by listing the situations that forty appears a pattern will appear:

1. The flood was forty days and forty nights.[2]
2. It took Moses forty days to received the Torah.[3]
3. Israel wondered forty years in the wilderness.[4]
4. Jesus fasted for forty days.[5]
5. And it was forty days from resurrection to ascension.[6]

Those are but a few of the examples, and already a pattern emerges. In every case in the Bible where the number forty occurs, time is being measured. Not only that, forty occurs when there is a paradigm shift or the cusp of something momentous.

The flood shows a transition from the age of creation to the age of patriarchs. (And if you look at the genealogies, you'll notice a precipitous drop in life expectancy shortly after the flood.) Forty days on the mountain marks the shift to the era of the Mosaic Law. Forty years of wandering transforms the Israelites from a band of runaway slaves into a conquering nation. Forty days of fasting transforms a Galilean carpenter into the Messiah. And forty days takes the world from a law of death to a royal law of love with the hope of resurrection.

So why is the number forty used to mark those changes? Is there anywhere in nature where the number forty is found? Yes! Just ask a mother. Gestation is forty weeks. It's as if God is pointing to something new. A new time, a new age, or a new phase in someone's life. It is the mark of conception and the birth of something great.

Chapter 3 Endnotes

[1] I Peter 3:20–21.
[2] Genesis 7:4.
[3] Exodus 24:18.
[4] Numbers 32:13.
[5] Matthew 4:2, Mark 1:13, and Luke 4:2.
[6] Acts 1:3.

4
Themes on Abram

The story of Abram is both wonderful and puzzling. Why was Abram chosen and not someone else? Could it be that many were called, but only Abram responded?

Nothing is known of his early life. He could have been, as tradition says, a pagan, or he and his family could have been from a long line of God-fearing worshipers. All that is known is that, late in Abram's life (75 to be exact[1]), he left all that he knew and let God direct him to a distant land.

Isn't it amazing that such a simple act would transform the world—and not just the religious world? Thomas Cahill, in his book *The Gift of the Jews*,[2] shows that, in many ways, western culture started with this journey of Abram. The western sense of justice, its concept of human rights, and its view of the universe started with Genesis 12.

Still, the question comes, why Abram? We have to be satisfied with God's statement, "I will have mercy on whom I will have mercy, and I will have compassion on whom I will have compassion."[3] In other words, why *not* Abram? As unsatisfying as it may be, God's plan had to start sometime with someone, and Abram is that person without explanation.

The first few chapters on Abram show a beautiful and unique aspect to the Bible—an aspect that can be viewed in almost musical terms. Like a great symphony or opera, some themes are introduced and later revisited with variations. Those themes work as harmonizing melodies that resonate throughout the composition giving it depth and power.

The first of those themes is God's promise to Abram. The promise is first given when Abram is called to leave his father's house and to go where God directs him. God pledges to bless him and make his name great, to make his descendents a mighty nation, and to give them the land of Canaan.[4] This promise is given three more times with variations; each time has greater power and force. The next time it is given with a blood covenant. This ritual may seem strange to modern man, but it was very serious to Abram's generation. By walking through that trench of blood between the cut carcasses, Abram was saying, "May this, and more, happen to me if I fail to fulfill my part of this covenant." The blazing torch passed through it was God tying Himself to the covenant with Abram.[5] The third time was with a pledge cut into Abram's own flesh with the act of circumcision.[6] Finally, came the greatest promise of all. God not only renewed His promise to Abraham but He added to it. God renewed the promise to make him the father of a many nations and to give his descendants the land of Canaan, but He also stated, for the first time, that through Abraham's seed "all nations on earth will be blessed." This promise came from Abraham's willingness to sacrifice his own son, Isaac, and to show His absolute sincerity, God swore by the greatest thing possible, Himself.[7]

Another theme, which appears later in Genesis and Matthew, is seeking refuge in Egypt.[8] It's interesting that Abraham is permitted to flee the land during famine, but Isaac is prohibited in a similar situation.[9] However, Jacob is sent to Egypt[10] with Moses later bringing the Israelites out. The final time has Joseph, Mary, and Jesus fleeing Herod.[11] Each time, the people were fleeing death. And each time, God led them out to greater glory. Isn't it strange how each exodus was by the chief person of the epoch? Abraham, the first of the patriarchs, goes down and returns with greater wealth and power than when he entered. When Moses comes out, Israel as a nation is given the Torah. When Jesus comes, the Messianic age has dawned, which brings a blessing to all the earth.

What is wonderful is how this theme so blends with the first—like two counter melodies played in unison, strengthening and harmonizing one another. Abraham's promise had three parts: to bless him and make his name great, to make his descendants a mighty nation able to take the land, and to sanctify the nations of the earth through his seed. Each part of that promise was fulfilled with a coming out of Egypt.

The final theme centers on Melchizedek. Here is a priest and a king; only one other person in the Bible holds both offices. Melchizedek was the king of Salem, and Salem means peace. Another will have the title Prince of Peace.[12] (Remember Jerusalem means city of peace. Melchizedek's Salem could've been Jerusalem.) Finally, Melchizedek means righteous king, and another righteous king will come.

Melchizedek is interesting because he is mentioned in only two other places in the Bible. The first is in the Psalms, and it is a messianic prophecy of the Messiah's priesthood.[13] The other is in Hebrews,[14] where the writer explains the superiority of the Melchizedek priestly order over the Aaron order because Abraham received Melchizedek's blessing. The person blessing is always viewed as superior to the one blessed. Moreover, Abraham tithed to Melchizedek, which again shows his subordinate position. And as the author of Hebrews pointed out, Aaron is lesser than Abraham because he is Abraham's descendant and, therefore, below Melchizedek. (I hope this summary of such a perfect and important passage in scripture was not too confusing. Hebrews should be read, studied, and remembered by all believers.)

The second part of Abraham's contact with Melchizedek is a motif often overlooked. It's similar to the baseline harmony of a symphony that's almost unnoticed. When Abraham meets Melchizedek, Lot had just been saved, and Melchizedek greets Abraham with bread and wine. How many times are rescue and destruction coupled with bread and wine? It is here in this passage with the rescue of Lot and the destruction of the four kings. It appears again with Joseph and the restoration of the cupbearer, along with the execution of the baker.[15] There is the tradition of wine and bread at the Passover, commemorating Israel's deliverance while Egypt lamented.[16] Last, and most important of all, the Last Supper[17] in which Christ's sacrifice rescues mankind from sin and removes death's dominion.

Chapter 4 Endnotes

[1] Genesis 12:4.
[2] Thomas Cahill, *The Gift of the Jews: How a Tribe of Nomads Changed the Way Everyone Thinks and Feels* (New York: Doubleday, 1998).
[3] Exodus 33:19.
[4] Genesis 12:7.
[5] Genesis 15:9–19.
[6] Genesis 17:5.
[7] Genesis 22:16–18.
[8] Genesis 12:10–20.
[9] Genesis 26:2.
[10] Genesis 46.
[11] Matthew 2:13.
[12] Isaiah 9:6.
[13] Psalms 110:4.
[14] Hebrew 5:1–7:28.
[15] Genesis 40:1–23.
[16] Exodus 12.
[17] Luke 22:19–20.

5

Why Was Ishmael Born?

The Bible speaks of many occasions in which God has complete control of man's procreation. It tells how He caused Abimelech's wives and concubines to become barren when Sarah was taken form Abraham.[1] Later, He opened the wombs of Rebekah,[2] Rachel,[3] and Hanna;[4] caused the virgin birth of Mary;[5] and caused the equally miraculous pregnancy of Sarah.[6]

With all of that power to allow who will and won't be born, one question should leap out. Why did God allow Ishmael to be born? Isaac was the child of promise, and of the many children of Abraham, he was the second son. God could have had Isaac born first but chose Ishmael. Why?

A complete survey of the Bible is required to fully appreciate why Ishmael was born. For this theme is so pronounced that it echoes throughout the Bible. The Bible constantly has pairings. There is Cain and Abel, Ishmael and Isaac, Esau and Jacob, Leah and Rachel, Manasseh and Ephraim, Saul and David, Elijah and Elisha, and finally John and Jesus.

In each case, a pattern emerges, sometimes striking and at other times so subtle it is hardly perceivable. Nonetheless, the pattern is there.

Cain came first, but Abel's sacrifice was more pleasing.[7]

As stated earlier, Isaac was the son of promise. His birth eventually caused Ishmael to be driven from the house of Abraham.[8] Although Ishmael became great in his own right, it was through Isaac that God's promises were fulfilled.

Another situation arose with Esau and Jacob. Esau was the older of the two, and he was Isaac's favorite. Everything should have been his, but Jacob supplanted him. With the two striving in the womb, it seemed almost preordained that Jacob would gain the birthright and the blessing.[9]

This pattern is seen again and again in Jacob's family. The first time is with his wives. Leah was his first wife, and by tradition, she held the greatest honor. However, Rachel was the one he loved. She was so loved that Leah had to bribe Rachel for a night with her husband.[10]

The next time is with Jacob's grandsons. When Joseph brought his two sons to be blessed, he made sure that Manasseh, the oldest, would have Jacob's right hand placed on his head. This ensured that the greater blessing was given to the oldest. But as the children approached, Jacob crossed his arms and placed his right hand on Ephraim, the youngest. When Joseph tried to have Jacob change the blessing, Jacob replied that Ephraim would become the greater of the two brothers.[11] Eventually, Ephraim became an endearing term to refer to all of Israel.

Saul was the first king of Israel; he was the one who took the people from tribal bands to a nation. By all rights, he should have been for Israel what George Washington was for America. But David was greater. David was anointed to replace Saul. Why should Saul ever be placed on the throne if David's dynasty was destined to rule?

Elijah may have been the more colorful prophet but recall what happened at his ascension in the fiery chariot. Elisha asked for, and received, a double portion of Elijah's spirit.[12]

John himself pointed out the pattern when he told his disciples that his decreasing to Jesus increasing was by heaven's design.[13]

In every case—whether by sacrifice, promise, ordainment, love, blessing, anointment, spirit, or prophecy—what came after surpassed what came before.

In the fourth chapter of Galatians, Paul gives a brilliant exposition of how Hagar and Sarah represent the old and new convent. He shows how Ishmael was a child of enslavement while Isaac, like the resurrection, came out of love, freedom, and inheritance. One was a servant, while the other was a son.

Paul reinforced that concept earlier when, in chapter 3, he said that all believers were children of Abraham. Which is greater, to be a child of the flesh or a child of the spirit?

The pattern holds with all of God's dealings. The world was first destroyed by water, but the second destruction will be with unquenchable fire. Man's first birth is by flesh, while his second is in spirit and water. Christ came first in humble surroundings as a simple carpenter, but He will return on the clouds in glory.

Consider this too: God made the angels before He made man. The angels rebelled first, and He turned them into demons as punishment.[14] Will not man's glory surpass the angels and his chastisement be more horrific than the demons?

Chapter 5 Endnotes

[1] Genesis 20:17–18.
[2] Genesis 25:21.
[3] Genesis 29:31.
[4] I Samuel 1:15 and 1:20.
[5] Matthew 1:20.
[6] Genesis 18.
[7] Genesis 2:4–5.
[8] Genesis 21:14.
[9] Genesis 25:22–27.
[10] Genesis 30:15.
[11] Genesis 48:19–21.
[12] II Kings 2:10–12.
[13] John 3:26–27.
[14] II Peter 2:4; Jude 1:6

6
Circumcision

Circumcision is an unusual, although not completely unique, custom. It has been practiced throughout Asia and Africa and in several Native American cultures. In most of those cultures, the serpent was seen as a holy symbol or a god, and circumcision was performed as a passage into manhood at puberty. Anthropologists believe it's a simulation of a snake shedding its skin and being renewed. Circumcision is seen as a method of striving for immortality.[1] If you consider the account of the serpent in the Garden, God was probably striving for a different symbolism when choosing circumcision as the sign of His covenant with Abraham.

The Jewish version has several marked contrasts from the pagan ritual. All males, including servants and slaves, were to submit to it. Circumcision wasn't a right of passage since infants were circumcised after their eighth day of birth. Those differences, though minor, are enough to make the custom something completely distinct from the rest of the world.

Look at how the term is used in scripture. Jeremiah spoke of uncircumcised ears not hearing God.[2] Moses referred to his speech impediment as "uncircumcised lips",[3] and Isaiah equates uncircumcision to being unclean.[4] In many passages, a godly soul was said to have a circumcised heart.[5] Stephen, before the Sanhedrin, accused the Jewish leaders of being uncircumcised in heart and ears—they were always resisting the Holy Spirit.[6] An uncircumcised man was shunned and viewed by the community as a foreigner.[7] Failure to submit to circumcision resulted in being cutoff from the nation and losing your family and everything. Those who wanted to join the Jewish faith had to agree to this ceremony. It sanctified men before God. Circumcision is what made one Jewish—not family, birth, blood, status, nor ancestry.

Meditate on circumcision, and some stunning things are noticed. It was literally a removing of flesh. It was performed on the eighth day of a child's life,[8] which is exactly one week after birth. Think back to the first chapter of Genesis and compare this act to the creation cycle. Circumcision was done on the start of a new creation cycle. A kind of rebirth occurs, which makes the child Jewish. Circumcision was also an emblem of one's devotion to God, but it was something that could not be openly displayed. It was also one of the most intimate and personal ways a man could connect to God. Circumcision echoes what Paul says in his call for Christian unity.[9] It is a part of the body that can be seen as shameful, and at the same time, it has the greatest need of protection. Yet, it is the most glorified and honored member of the body.

When looking at circumcision as a whole, there is obviously a parallel in Christianity. It is a ceremony that spiritually sanctifies, making one a spiritual child of Israel, and shows a rebirth by putting away the flesh. It is the humble submission of baptism.

Baptism is a symbolic removal of flesh that allows the spirit to live. It is a symbolic rebirth that sanctifies us before God, and it is a humiliation—by the world's sense of reasoning—that allows an intimate relationship to God. Baptism sanctifies and places us into spiritual Israel.

Remember that baptism is not a Christian invention. The ceremonial cleansing of washing away the old self was first a Jewish ceremony known as Mikvah. Baptism is part of the ceremony that would bring a gentile into the Jewish nation. In fact, it was the final act by men and women who were proselytized.

This is why John's baptism was so shocking to the Pharisees and scribes. John was saying that God's love and grace were no one's birthright. It was the highest insult possible to tell those self-righteous men that they were no different from the gentiles. It is no small wonder that he was so hated.

Some in the Christian community balk at the idea of baptism. They point to Paul's eloquent rebuttal to circumcision in Galatians while ignoring the many references, allusions, and out right statements of baptism in his other writings. They declare baptism as trivial because Christ didn't baptize.[10] But they forget that His disciples baptized and were baptized.[11] They even ignore that Christ showed the way by being baptized when he had no need of it.[12]

The question of justification is the only point that doesn't rest on sophomoric argument or shoddy logic. Christians are justified by faith and not by works. Salvation can only be seen as a gift of God's grace, and man can never boast of his works. Any Christian who argues that his salvation is assured by his baptism is a fool. For Christians to place their justification in baptism is just as mistaken as the Pharisees who placed their justification on circumcision. Scripture is too explicitly clear for debate.

Scripture is equally explicit in the Messianic commandment to go and baptize.[13] Attempts to wipe it away with legalistic logic are on par with Pharisaic traditions that negated the weightier elements of the Torah.

Thousands of pages have been written that deal with Greek linguistics, grammar, and definitions on whether one is baptized *because* of remission of sins or to *gain* remission of sin. The debate has been run to the ground many times, and it is all a red herring!

In the end, the humble obedient heart is what matters. Can anyone claim to have such a heart if he refuses to obey the simple command of baptism? Is not the sinner's refusal of baptism a way of saying he will come to God only on his own terms and not God's? By refusing baptism are you not rejecting Christ's example and claiming to be better than Christ?

Chapter 6 Endnotes

[1] Desmond Morris, Babywatching (New York: Crown Publishing, 1992), p. 193.
[2] Jeremiah 6:10 (King James Version).
[3] Exodus 6:12 (King James Version).
[4] Isaiah 52:1.
[5] Jeremiah 4:4.
[6] Acts 7:51.
[7] Genesis 17:14.
[8] Leviticus 12:3.
[9] I Corinthians 12:23–24.
[10] John 4:2.
[11] John 3:22.
[12] Matthew 3:15
[13] Matthew 28:18–20.

7
What Could Have Saved Sodom and Gomorrah?

The story of Sodom and Gomorrah is one that is wedged into the biblical narrative that makes one wonder why it's even there. God abhors immorality and sin. So why expand on the destruction of two minor cities lost in the mist of time?

Historically, people tend to stress the sins of Sodom. In the past, moralists used the Sodomites call for Lot's guest as justification in criminalizing homosexuality. Today, apologists of the gay community stress the inhospitality of the Sodomites call for rape as the key sin.

Both arguments have a certain force, but they lack some creditability. Homosexuality and abuse of the sojourner are condemned in Mosaic teaching. And throughout history, there were societies guilty of both, but they did not fall under the direct judgment of God. So why were Sodom and Gomorrah different? Why were those cities destroyed by God personally and no others?

The point of the story is not Sodom and Gomorrah but God's conversation with Abraham. Abraham convinced God to spare the righteous even at the cost of justice. He started at fifty righteous souls and bargained God down to ten; a little goodness can go along way to save the wicked. The story shows that God will stay His executing hand for the sake of the righteous![1]

This story is a companion to the flood and the final judgment. In all those cases, man's wickedness reached the point of absolute. The Bible stresses that the mob that called for the strangers was "all" the men from every quarter of the city.[2] Just as in Noah's time, the whole city was entirely evil. And as with Noah, only the righteous escaped. The story also shows what is to come—destruction not with water but with fire. It is a prototype of the last day, and like the last day, only the righteous are saved. However, not all who could be among the righteous were saved. Lot's sons-in-law chose to stay,[3] and his wife turned back to the city.[4] Those decisions are a kind of parable about the nature of sin. There are those capable of salvation, like the sons-in-law, who reject the offer of salvation. And there are also those, like the wife, who are saved but return to sin.

The teachings of Christ expound on this story. What springs to mind is the Sermon on the Mount, where He tells the righteous that they "are the salt of the earth."[5] Salt is a preservative. In like manner, the righteous preserve the world from God's justice, for God will not "kill the righteous with the wicked."[6] If ever the world becomes thoroughly evil in all its quarters, there will be no staying God's executing hand.

Chapter 7 Endnotes

[1] Genesis 18:16–33.
[2] Genesis 19:4.
[3] Genesis 19:14.
[4] Genesis 19:26.
[5] Matthew 5:13.
[6] Genesis 18:25.

8

Isaac on the Altar

The sacrifice of Isaac is one of the pivotal points in the Jewish and Christian faith. It is the climax of the Abrahamic story, with the three key elements of Abraham, Isaac, and the location of the sacrifice.[1]

What Abraham symbolizes should be obvious. His placing Isaac on the altar is seen as a God-like act that points to the Messiah. His willingness to sacrifice his beloved and promised son is the easiest and first thing noticed in this story. But more than his willingness is the condition of his heart—the true concern of God. Once Abraham accepted God's command, in his heart Isaac was already dead. Placing him on the altar and slitting his throat were frivolous extensions. During that three-day journey, Abraham grieved for his dead son; the son he had already sacrificed in his mind and heart. When God stayed his hand, Abraham already had Isaac in his tomb. In Abraham's heart, it was a resurrection from the dead.

Isaac is an often overlooked part of the story. Most writers and preachers emphasize Abraham, but Isaac is more than a passive addition to the story. His participation is as crucial as Abraham's and is just as symbolic. Here is a child, a young man actually, taken to a mountain top and literally placed under the condemnation of death. He is prepared to have his father spill his blood, but another takes his place. A ram with his horns caught in the bush is placed on the altar. This "lamb of God" was provided to have its blood shed instead.[2] Isaac is a metaphor for humanity!

Consider where the sacrifice occurred. Scripture says the "region of Moriah,"[3] and Jewish tradition places it on top of Mount Moriah. This hilltop pops up several times in Israelite history. The next time it's mentioned is during the reign of David.[4] Satan "stirred David's heart" to have a census of the fighting men of Israel. This act was despicable because David was placing his faith in the might of his army rather than the power of God. As the story unfolds, God unleashes three days of pestilence on Israel for David's impertinence. The Angel of Death was standing at the threshing floor of Araunah the Jebusite stretching out his hand to destroy Jerusalem when God said, "Enough!" Immediately afterwards, the prophet Gad instructed David to erect an altar to God on that same threshing floor. The altar was built at the top of Mount Moriah, and the hilltop is where Solomon built the temple.[5]

Isn't it interesting that God's temple would be at a place that once winnowed grain. After all, the temple could be seen as a place where God's winnowing fork separates the wheat and chaff of men's souls.[6] At its foundation was a peace offering to God begging forgiveness for man's sinful pride and rejoicing at the stay of execution. Deeper still to the foundation was an offering of a righteous son of anointed promise.

The Christian temple has similar sacrifices laid at its foundation. The Christian body is now the house of God. At the foundation is the Christian's living sacrifice, and before that is the holy offering of the promised Son who became sin.

Chapter 8 Endnotes

[1] Genesis 22:1–19.
[2] Genesis 22:13.
[3] Genesis 22:2.
[4] II Samuel 24.
[5] II Chronicles 3:1.
[6] Matthew 3:12 and Luke 3:17.

9
Meeting Your Bride at the Well

Another theme repeated in the Torah, with variations, is meeting your bride at the well. Robert Alter's excellent discourse lays out the general pattern of these stories.[1] A stranger comes to the well; a young woman (usually beautiful) is either there to draw water for the family or their sheep. She or the stranger needs help to draw water from the well, and then the woman runs home in excitement. The head of the house meets the man, and after some negotiations, the woman and the stranger are betrothed.

Like a musical theme repeated in an opera, this story is repeated three times in the Torah. The first time, the stranger was Abraham's servant that was sent to find a wife for Isaac, and the woman was Rebekah.[2] This meeting sets the pattern perfectly in every way. But, it has one thing more. With the servant asking for God's guidance in finding the right woman, and then receiving the sign he requested so completely in Rebekah, it showed that the match was God directed and blessed. This situation implies that all such meetings were directed and blessed by God.

The second occurrence is when Jacob meets Rachel.[3] This story has a slight variation in that he is the one watering her sheep. It also has the added difficulty in that he has to roll back a stone covering the well. (Scripture hints that this act was an amazing task). As before, a negotiation was made for the bride. But where Laban took gold for his sister, he requires seven years of labor for his daughter. Although not exactly as Jacob had intended, the deceiver was himself deceived, and Jacob ended up giving fourteen years for two wives.

The next time is with Moses.[4] Here, as with Jacob, he is running for his life. With Jacob, it was Esau, and with Moses, it was Pharaoh. Once again, the stranger meets his bride at the well, but this time she is one among many. (Reuel had seven daughters, and Zipporah was one of them.)

Like Jacob, Moses aids his bride, but this time, he has to rescue her from the shepherds that drove her and her sisters away. This leads to him being taken in by Reuel's family and given his bride. Although it doesn't say it outright, the story suggests that like Rebekah and Rachel, Zipporah was pure and beautiful.

As is seen in each case, the pattern is repeated. A stranger meets a young woman at the well—and if not stated outright, it is at least suggested that she is virtuous and pure—and for a price, she is secured as a bride (either for the stranger or his master). However, there is one variation that should be noted. Each time becomes more difficult and more dangerous. The first time, there is only a simple request for water, the second time a stone must be rolled away from the well, and the third time the suitor must rescue his bride.

The story is repeated one more time: in the Gospel of John, where the Messiah meets the Samaritan woman at Jacob's well.[5] There are similarities and variations between this incident and the others. Like the others, they met at a well and water was given. She was so excited that she left her water jar behind and ran to the city to tell the men about Jesus, and the men came out to bring him back to the city and show him the hospitality of a guest. Many will say, yes that's all true but he didn't marry her. She was far from virtuous with five ex-husbands and living in sin. True, Jesus doesn't marry her—yet. Bear in mind that the church is the Bride of Christ, and just as Hosea's adulteress wife, Gomer,[6] was the perfect metaphor for Israel, this woman symbolizes the church. She was a Samaritan, half Jewish and half Gentile. So is the church with the separating wall broken down[7] all are sons of Abraham, whether by birth or adoption. And like the church, she too was marred by sin and desperately needing salvation and redemption.

Jesus meeting her also parallels the other stories, with some variation. Just as the servant asked for water from Rebekah and gave her betrothal gifts, so Jesus asked for water and gave the woman the bridal gift of living water. In the same fashion, as Jacob had to roll the stone form the well to water Rachel's flock, the Lord had to roll the stone from the woman's heart so she could draw the living water from within Him. And like Moses, Jesus has to rescue his bride. But where Moses had to rescue her from malicious shepherds, Jesus must rescue His bride from sin.

One final thought. As was mentioned earlier, each time the intensity was increased. The servant had to bear gifts; Jacob had to perform the formidable task of moving the stone and then labor for seven years; and Moses had to fight off shepherds. Jesus had to sacrifice Himself to gain His bride. Through that sacrifice He turns a disreputable, ugly hag into a bride as pure and beautiful as Rebekah, Rachel, and Zipporah.

Chapter 9 Endnotes

[1] <u>The Art of Biblical Narrative</u>, Robert Alter, Basic Books, 1981, page 52
[2] Genesis 24:10-57
[3] Genesis 29:1-28
[4] Exodus 2:15–22.
[5] John 4:4–42.
[6] Hosea 1:2.
[7] Ephesians 2:14.

10
Joseph and Judah

Why is so much of Genesis devoted to the story of Joseph? It surpasses even the stories of Abraham, Isaac, and Jacob in the amount of detail. So why would God spend so much time and effort on Joseph's story?

A quick review of Joseph's life may give some insight. Recall that Joseph was a beloved son. In fact, he was Jacob's favorite son. Jacob even placed Joseph above his elder brothers, and his brothers hated Joseph for telling the truth about them to their father.[83] To make matters worse, Jacob gave Joseph a coat of many colors. It was so richly adorned that only princes or kings would wear one like it. Then to completely consummate his brothers' hatred, Joseph tells them that God has chosen him to be the greatest of all—even greater than their own father! That was the obvious meaning of his dreams.[84] No wonder his brothers hated him enough to want him dead.

However, they didn't want his blood on their hands. So they handed him over to a group of foreigners to do their dirty work. Make no mistake—selling Joseph into slavery was tantamount to a death sentence. Moreover, they were paid very well for his innocent blood.

By going down into Egypt, Joseph was reduced from a prince to a slave. Although he rose to prominence in Potifer's house, he was still a slave!

Joseph maintained his righteousness and was so trusted that his master gave him complete control of the whole household. Then once again, Joseph falls victim to the evil of others. He is falsely accused and is reduced even lower to criminal status.

While in prison, he meets the pharaoh's baker and cupbearer. It is interesting that, once again, the sub-theme of bread and wine coupled with death and salvation is joined with the theme of restoration after three days (as it was with Isaac). It's through the cupbearer that Joseph is not only released from prison but also raised to a glory higher than he had ever, or could ever, achieve.

Then for the final irony, he is there to save the very ones that caused his degradation. To use his own words, "You intended to harm me, but God intended it for good to accomplish what is now being done, the saving of many lives."[85]

This quick review of Joseph's life should make it obvious that he is a precursor of the Messiah. All of the main points are there: Joseph, a prince, is (a) degraded and from that degradation obtains a higher glory, (b) betrayed for a price and handed over to foreigners, and (c) risen up to save those who betrayed him. All of this took years but was directed by God from the beginning.

Many see those parallels very quickly, but there is another aspect of the story that is often overlooked. Most people forget about Joseph's brothers, particularly the details of his four eldest brothers.

At first, Ruben appears to be a hero. He is the one who talks the others out of killing Joseph. Ruben plans to rescue the boy and return him to Jacob, but when he finds Joseph missing, his first concern is for himself.[86] Ruben needed to get back in his father's good graces because of a shameful act he had done earlier: he laid with Bilhahy, Jacob's concubine.[87] Although that act was before the Law, it was still a shameful act. Paul wrote of a similar situation that occurred at the church in Corinth, and he said it was something so shameful that it wasn't done even among the pagans.[88] Remember that was Corinth, which was the most sexually charged city of the ancient world; its patron god was Aphrodite; and almost every sexual perversion wasn't just permitted but encouraged. Ruben's sin against God and Israel was so grievous that he lost his birthright. Like Esau, he gave up his birthright for the flesh. Worse still, he never realized his own sinfulness. Later, Ruben blamed his brother's actions against Joseph for causing their problems in Egypt.[89] Not once did he consider his own sins as the cause of God's punishment.

When Ruben lost his birthright, it should have gone to the next son. However, both Simeon and Levi (the next two sons) had brought shame to God and their father. Recall that Shechem the Hivite had violated their sister, Dinah.[90] Although the Bible implies it was as much a willing seduction on her part as rape on his part, to Shechem's credit, he was willing to make her his wife. He was so willing in fact that he and all his people submitted to circumcision as part of the marriage contract. In place of Shechem's sincerity, Simeon and Levi acted deceitfully.[91] From the beginning, their plan was to use the holy convent of circumcision to kill Shechem and to massacre his town. When Jacob confronts them, they justify themselves by blaming Shechem for their sinful actions. The shame they brought on God and Jacob made them ineligible to receive the birthright when Ruben lost it.

With the three eldest disqualified, the birthright fell to Judah. However, Judah wasn't any better than his brothers. He was the one who wanted to sell Joseph to the Ishmaelites,[92] and he shows himself as an even greater reprobate regarding Tamar.[93] Judah completely disregards custom and law by denying Tamar the right of children. Later, he consorts with who he thinks is a temple prostitute but who is really Tamar. Once she is pregnant, Judah is prepared to have her burned to death for the sake of family honor.[94] This incident is the turning point in Judah's life, because once Tamar proves the children are his, Judah recognizes his own wickedness. He calls her the more righteous and places her under his protection. He could have denied his sin and hidden his shame by killing Tamar—no one would have known. Instead, he chose the harder and correct path.

Judah's change was more than cosmetic or a show for society—it was a change that went to the very heart. This change is apparent later during the second journey to Egypt. Judah was the one who guaranteed Benjamin's safety.[95] He was ready to guarantee it with something far more important than his life or even the lives of his sons. When he said, "I will bear the blame before you all my life," he was willing to accept his father's curse, which is no small matter when considering the lengths Jacob went to steal Esau's blessing. Judah further shows his complete change when he offers himself in Benjamin's place to become Joseph's slave.[96] This offer was enormous since Judah was free to go home, and he had no reason to suspect that Benjamin was innocent.

It was only after Joseph recognized this change that he reveled himself and was reunited with his family.

This change of heart made Judah worthy of the birthright that passed from Abraham to Isaac to Jacob and now to Judah. This transformation is why the Messiah was from the tribe of Judah and not Ruben.

Chapter 10 Endnotes

[1] Genesis 37:2.
[2] Genesis 37:5–10.
[3] Genesis 50:20.
[4] Genesis 37:21, 29.
[5] Genesis 35:22.
[6] I Corinthians 5:1.
[7] Genesis 42:22.
[8] Genesis 34.
[9] Genesis 34:13.
[10] Genesis 37:26.
[11] Genesis 38.
[12] Genesis 38:24.
[13] Genesis 43:8–10.
[14] Genesis 44:18–34.

11

The Jewish Iliad

The story of Exodus is one of the greatest epic stories of all time. Exodus is for the Jews what the *Iliad* is for the Greeks, the *Aeneid* for the Romans, the *Song of Roland* for the French, the *Legend of the Cid* for the Spaniards, and the *Arthurian Tales* for the British. It is the story that unites the Jews and sets them as a unique people among the nations of the world.

Because it stands with those other epic stories and is the oldest, some people assume that it is no different from its peers. Most of the modern world assumes that its roots are in distant history but that its final fruit is more myth than history. They are wrong! Exodus doesn't fit in the paradigm of mythology. For example, the Spartans claimed to be descended from Hercules. What nation would take pride from being a race of slaves who were incapable of freeing themselves? The very narrative is counter to other epics. In the Iliad and the Odyssey, the gods are supporting characters to the heroes Achilles and Odysseus. But in Exodus, God not Moses is the hero. Those differences point to a narrative unique in humanity. If Exodus was a mere invention of man, then it would show the Israelites in a far more positive and heroic light. It is the first attempt at recording human history and more. It is God's use of history to explain the nature of things and to point to what is to come. The Exodus is not myth and it is more than history.

Exodus is of great importance. Only the Gospels hold more significance to the Christian faith. Exodus is rich in metaphors and symbols that are only explained in light of the Messiah's life and His church.

It's easy to see the story of the Israelites mirroring the struggles of the Christian soul in the spiritual world. In the beginning, they are slaves in a foreign land, just as Christians are slaves to sin. The Israelites had to be saved by the might of God battling against the powers of the land. Likewise, Christians are redeemed not by their own strength but by God's gracious wish to save them (as Paul shows in his epistle to the Romans). Both are saved from enslaving forces through a watery rescue: the Israelites with the parting of the Red Sea and Christians by baptism.[1]

Exodus is not the end but the beginning of a new life where Jews and Christians are taken into the wilderness For the Israelites, it was a forty-year journey that destroyed a generation; for the Christian it's a lifetime of learning and devotion. The result is the same—the burning away of the old slave!

While wandering in the wilderness of this world, Christians show the same weaknesses as the Israelites. Christians look fondly at the time of slavery and wish to return to flesh pots of their past lives. They succumb to following the "golden calves" of prestige and affluence. Like Israel, Christians too will know the discipline of a loving father. In the end, the old man is gone and a new one is ready to enter a promise land that is awarded to the wanderer who remains faithful.

If Israel is the physical to what the Christian is to the spiritual then obviously Moses is the Christ for Israel. (This revelation is not shocking since the Torah states that a prophet like Moses would come some day.[2]) The parallels are as striking as it was for Israel. Both Moses and Jesus were princes who did not see royalty as something to be grasped, but instead chose to accept the plight of their brothers in slavery.[3] Both were rejected: Moses by the arguing Israelites who threatened to reveal his killing of a taskmaster and Jesus by the Pharisees who called his removal of our taskmaster the work of Beelzebub.[4] Both led ex-slaves into a wandering; one felt the exasperation of a grumbling people, while the other feels the pain of backsliding souls. In the end, Moses looks from a mountain top into the promise land but can never enter. Meanwhile, Jesus foretold of the Rock that was the foundation of His church, but He wasn't present to see it rise on Pentecost. Neither man has a tomb for the faithful to worship before. Moses' grave is unknown, and Jesus' grave is empty.

You should consider one final episode, and then the image is complete. Recall that on the Mountain of God while Moses was receiving the covenant that the Israelites were making the golden calf and preparing to return to slavery. It was at this point that God was ready to wipe them out and to fulfill His promise to Abraham through Moses. However, Moses interceded and turned away God's wrath.[5] What Moses did physically for Israel in saving their lives Jesus does spiritually for the Christian; He turns away God's wrath!

The Humble Man

The Torah refers to Moses as the humblest man on the face of the earth.[6] By tradition and faith, Moses is accepted as the author (or at least the scribe) of the Torah. So how could a humble man refer to himself as the humblest man alive?

He was merely stating fact by pointing out that he never used his position to aggrandize himself. He never required the Israelites to give him any of their wealth or flocks, and whenever they opposed him, he begged them not to arouse God's anger. Unlike Samuel, who God had to remind that the people's demand for a king was not a rejection of Samuel but of God,[7] Moses never took their complaints personally. (Well, almost never. One time, in his exasperation, he placed himself with God.) This humbleness is highlighted when the seventy elders had the spirit of the Lord pour out on them. When two stayed back in the camp and began to prophesy, Joshua ran to report them to Moses. When he heard this, Moses replied, "Are you jealous for my sake? I wish that all the Lord's people were prophets and that the Lord would put his Spirit on them!"[8] He was truly humble because he never considered himself as something to be grasped. His whole being was placed on the will of God.

Such humility would have to be the mark of the prophet to come that was foretold at the end of the Torah as being one like Moses. He would have to be one who, when His disciples reported that when they saw a man casting out demons in His name, they told the man to stop, would reply, "Do not stop him, for whoever is not against you is for you."[9] He would be a prophet willing to wash His own disciples' feet[10] and would tell them that the least of them was the greatest and that the last was the first.[11]

Chapter 11 Endnotes

[1] I Corinthians 10:1–3.
[2] Deuteronomy 18:15.
[3] Hebrews 11:24-25
[4] Matthew 12:24.
[5] Exodus 32:9–14
[6] Numbers 12:3.
[7] I Samuel 8:7.
[8] Numbers 11:29.
[9] Luke 9:49–50.
[10] John 13:4–5.
[11] Mark 9:33–37.

12

I AM!

The passages and phrases from the calling of Moses still influence Western thought like no other poetry of the era. "Burning bushes" are still seen as allusions for divine instruction, and the greatest are the humble who are called to higher glory against their will.

Moses is the epitome of the reluctant hero. Even when selected by God, and granted power and authority, Moses attempts to reject it. He never sees himself as the right man for the job despite his unique experience and knowledge. Moses grew up in the Egyptian court. He saw firsthand court politics and probably knew many of the key players. He may have even known the current pharaoh. Still, he tried to convince God that others were better suited for the task. Perhaps it was his intimate knowledge of the court that made him so reluctant. He knew what happened to those who opposed the king, and he saw no reason to trade his happy, simple life for the intrigues of power politics.

Recall what has happened to Moses up to this point. Moses, wishing to relieve the misery of his fellow Israelites, kills a cruel Egyptian taskmaster. But his own countrymen not only failed to appreciate his actions, they resented his position. That resentment cost him his princely place and forced him to flee for his life.

Moses fled to the land of Midian and worked as a shepherd for his father-in-law. While tending the flock, he witnessed on Mount Horeb a burning bush that was not consumed by the fire.[1] He investigates, and what he finds changes not only him but also history. Moses is given his ordainment to free God's people.

The first part of Moses' commission is a revelation so paramount that the very structure of the scripture is used to highlight it. This charge is another example of a chiasmus,[2] which is a convention in which the central theme is framed by other points that reflect back and highlight the focal point of the passage. Starting from the outside and working inward, you can easily see the heart of this scripture.

The first thing God proclaims is His awareness. He shows that He isn't an unfeeling god or a remote god. He is deeply concerned about His people and has the power and the will to change their condition. What is often seen as God's failure to act is nothing more than His setting the stage for His actions to have the greatest impact. God is, above all, a God of efficiency. The teacher is best when the student is ready to learn, and the artist is best when the audience is attentive with anticipation. When God fails to give it is usually because people are not ready to receive.

In verse 7, God tells how He has seen the suffering of Israel and has heard their cries. He will now rescue them from their oppressors. The reflection is from verse 18 to the end of the chapter. God tells how He will stretch out His hand to compel Pharaoh to let Israel go. In doing so, the Hebrews will plunder Egypt as the wages of their labor.

On the second-level chiasmus, God discloses His plan for Israel. In verse 8, He tells of giving them the "land of milk and honey," which is the land of the Amorites, Hittites, Hivites, Jebusites, and Pesizzites. To emphasize this plan, God states it again in verse 17. With this, He shows that it is time to begin fulfilling His promise to Abraham.

The third level is set in verses 10 and 16. Here God orders Moses to bring himself before Pharaoh (verse 10), the man who currently holds authority over the Israelites and enslaves them. The chiasmus is then reflected in God telling Moses to gather the elders (verse 16), the men who will hold authority and shepherd the children of God.

Now comes the heart of the revelation—the name of God! But even this eye-opener is framed. In verses 12 and 13, Moses asked God to give His name, and in verse 15, God says it is to be, "His name forever in memorial to all generations."

Now look at the whole:

Verse 7—I see your affliction.
    Verses 8-9—I will bring you to the promise land.
        Verse 10—You will stand before Pharaoh.
            Verses 12 and 13—What is your Name?
                Verse 14—I AM!
            Verse15—This name is mine forever.
        Verse 16—You will stand before the elders.
    Verse 17—I will bring you to the promise land.
Verse 18—I will strike Egypt for your affliction.

Thirty-five hundred years later, some of the power of this revelation has been lost due to its familiarity. But at the time, it was a thunder bolt. In *The Gift of the Jews*, Thomas Cahill gives a beautiful rendition of this story and explains its full implications.[3]

God's name is unique from all names in that it is a verb—the verb "to be." He emphasizes this usage by using the term "I AM" three times. More than that, Hebrew has a certain nuance that is lacking in English. There are three ways it can be viewed, and they are not necessarily mutually exclusive. "I AM" can be seen as God saying, "I am the root of everything. All that is, springs from Me." It can also be viewed as God saying, "I am always there for you. Fear not for I will never desert you." The third and final meaning is, "Who I am is none of your business because it is beyond your comprehension." This last meaning may seem a tad harsh, but it is imperative for human understanding. In ancient times, and even today, people tried to place God into human obligation. People thought that by performing specific ceremonies and speaking certain words that the gods would be forced to behave beneficially to human desires. God was letting Moses know that humanity can approach God only on God's terms and not on human terms. Jesus drove that point home in His parable about separating the sheep and the goats.[4] The goats were shocked that, in spite of their works and calling on His name, the Lord still rejected them.

In saying, "I AM who I AM, tell them I AM sent you," God seems to be using all three aspects of the term.

There is another unusual feature about "I AM"! In Hebrew, the term forms the tetragraph YHWH (translated into the Latin alphabet). This tetragraph can also be made from splicing portions of three Hebrew terms: "He who was," "He who is," and "He who will be."[5] God's very name demonstrates His eternal being and consistency.

Christians are not surprised with so many threes-in-one being intertwined in the meaning of YHWH Why shouldn't the name YHWH express the nature of God being three and yet one?

The Hebrew tetragraph YHWH is often pronounced Yahweh. But its true pronunciation is unknown because it hasn't been spoken in almost 2,000 years. It was only spoken on the Day of Atonement, and then just by the priest in the Holy of Holies. It was, and is, a name so precious to the Jews that when it is read aloud they substitute the word "Lord" in its place. When sofers, or scribes, are transcribing the Torah and come to this name, they will stop, pray, ceremonially cleanse themselves, and then write the name with a special pen that they use only to write those four letters.[6]

This reverence is a far cry from how Christians treat God's name. Yet, it is hard to say which treatment is better or more correct. The Jewish way is highly respectful, but that respect makes God distant, remote, and unapproachable. The Christian familiarity may not have the same level of dignity, but it allows a loving closeness given in the endearment "Abba Father."

Perhaps it is the tendency of placing God in such fearful remoteness that He chose to make His name a verb for being. When God is made too remote, it is easy to think that He is not there and, hence, the need to have His name emphasize that He Is!

The translation of YHWH to Yahweh assumes a two-syllable pronunciation. But if the tetragraph is pronounced as one syllable without the vowels, it becomes a forced breath pushed outward. It is interesting that God's name may be a breath, especially when so much of scripture ties breath and spirit together.

In many languages, the root of breath and spirit is the same. In Japanese, for example, the word for spirit is "ki," and the shout to force air out of the lungs is "kiai." Zecharia Sitchin, in his book *Genesis Revisited*,[7] points out that in the ancient Sumerian language (of which Hebrew is an offshoot) the words "wind," "breath," and "spirit" have the same root. Genesis 1:2 could just as easily be translated as God's breath was blown over the void. Breathing the breath of life into man is placing the spirit into man. The rushing wind of Pentecost[8] can be seen as God breathing out and placing a renewed spirit into man. A spirit, like the burning bush, that set the Apostles on fire, but did not consume them. A breath in them, and every Christian, that unites them with I AM and still allows them to be separate and individual.

The second part of Moses' ordainment is receiving authority, which is chronicled in the first half of chapter 4. Moses knows that Pharaoh and the Israelites will require proof and, God willingly gives him three signs to demonstrate before them—signs that foreshadow a greater prophet to come. (Notice how often the number three appears when dealing with God.)

The first sign was Moses casting his staff down and it changing into a serpent.[9] Moses first flees from it, but at God's command, he takes it by the tail and it becomes his staff again. This points forward to the Messiah and backward toward Eve. The Messiah, like Moses, will confront the serpent, but where Moses takes it by the tail to control it the Messiah's heel will crush its head to conquer it.

The second sign was Moses placing his hand into his bosom. The hand turns leprous and then is healed.[10] Once more, this points to the Messiah. Leprosy was viewed as unclean, and uncleanliness was (and is) synonymous with sin. This sign pointed to the one who would cleanse the world of sin.

The final sign of water turning into blood when poured on the ground hints at the coming sacrifice of the Messiah.[11] It is also a precursor to the first plague in Egypt and the Messiah's first miracle of turning water into wine.[12] Interesting how the ministry of Christ parallels Moses' mission. The first plague turned water to blood, which set in motion the freeing of Israel from Egyptian slavery. The Messiah's first miracle of turning water into wine started a ministry that would free the world from sinful slavery.

Regardless of all those signs of authority, Moses still wanted God to choose someone else. He tried time and time again to convince God that he wasn't the right man. Moses wanted the cup to pass from him. Here again Moses' and Jesus' lives parallel. Both begged the Father to have the cup pass,[13] but in the end both—as do all who seek to be God's servants— had no choice but to accept God's will.

The Lord Bless You and Keep You

Chapter 6 versus 24–25 of Numbers is one of the best-known passages of the Bible. It has been heard so many times that it's often reviewed without really thinking about it. But contemplate it for a moment.

"May the Lord bless you and keep you.
May the Lord's face shine upon you and be gracious unto you.
May the Lord lift His countenance on you and give you peace."

Consider that "the Lord" is actually the Hebrew tetra graph YHWH that is translated as "I AM." Also recall that I AM can have three very different connotations, so that blessing could be translated as the following:

"May I AM who is the source of everything, protect you and make you His.
May I AM who is always there, delight in you and forgive your transgressions.
May I AM who is beyond your comprehension; give you the serenity of His approval. "

From the Christian view of God, this blessing has an even different perspective:

"May the Father love you and make you His child.
May the Son be a shining light guiding your way to redemption.
May the Holy Spirit come into you heart and give the utterances and groans of your soul a voice to the Almighty God."

Chapter 12 Endnotes

[1] Exodus 3:2.
[2] John Dart, "Scriptural Schemes: The ABCBAs of Biblical Writing," *Christian Century*, July 13, 2004.
[3] Thomas Cahill, *The Gift of the Jews: How a Tribe of Desert Nomads Changed the Way Everyone Thinks and Feels* (New York: Doubleday, 1998), pp. 108–16.
[4] Matthew 25:31–46.
[5] Aryeh Kaplan, *The Handbook of Jewish Thought, Volume 2* (New York: Moznaim Publishing Corp., 1992).
[6] PBS Religion and Ethics, "Torah Restoration," Episode 247, July 23, 1999.
[7] Sitchin, Zecharia, *Genesis Revisited: Is Modern Science Catching Up with Ancient Knowledge?* (Rochester: VT: Bear and Company, 1991).

I do not recommend Sitchin's book in any way, shape, or form. Although, it gives on occasion some insight to ancient languages and culture, its overall thesis is at best blasphemous.

[8] Acts 2:2.
[9] Exodus 4:3–4.
[10] Exodus 4:6–7.
[11] Exodus 4:9.
[12] John 2:3–10.
[13] Matthew 26:39.

13
God's War

As an experiment, make a list of the Egyptian gods or the various things the Egyptians worshiped. A quick search on the Internet could be helpful.

Now the Egyptian pantheon is not as easily laid out as the Greek and Roman pantheons. Most of this is because Egypt is a more ancient. Many deities came and went depending on the dynasty and the Pharaoh. However, certain gods were consistently worshiped throughout Egypt's long history.[1]

Among them was Seth, god of storms and chaos. Another prominent god was Ra (or Aman-Re) the sun god. There was Osiris, god of vegetation. and agriculture . Egyptians also worshiped Apis and Hathor, bull god and cow goddess. (In fact, there were special Apis bulls who were treated as living gods among the Egyptians and were mummified after their deaths.) There was Hapi, god of the Nile; Geb, god of earth; Heket, the frog goddess; Khepri, goddess of the blue beetles; Amon and Shu, gods of the winds; Nut, god of the sky; Isis, goddess of healing; Imhotep, god of medicine; and Anubis, god of death. Pharaoh's rule was justified by the people accepting him as being divine, and Horus, the hawk god and child of Osiris and Isis, was tied directly to the Pharaoh. This list is just a few of their numerous gods, but many of the primary ones.

Now list the plagues. They were the following: the Nile turning to blood, being overrun by frogs, gnats springing from the ground, flies (or other insects) swarming, livestock becoming diseased, festering boils, damaging hail, devouring locust, overwhelming darkness, and finally the Angel of Death killing all firstborn.

Now compare the two lists. Their similarities should be strikingly self-evident. Every plague corresponds to one or more of the Egyptian gods: the Nile to Hapi; frogs to Heqet, gnats to Geb; flies (or insects) to Khepri;

livestock to Apis and Hathor; boils to Isis, Imhotep, and Pharaoh; hail to Seth, and Osiris; locust to Amon and Shu; darkness to Ra and Nut; and finally death to Anubis.

The plagues were neither attacks on the Egyptian people nor just on Pharaoh's heart. The attack was on the gods of Egypt. God was showing the Egyptians and, more important, the Israelites that He was supreme. He could not only match but also supersede any god—even in that god's own domain. He was demonstrating what Paul would later state, "If God is for us who can be against us?"[2] And the plagues shout out, "No one! Not even other gods!"

Chapter 13 Endnotes

[1] Wilkinson, Richard H., *The Complete Gods and Goddesses of Ancient Egypt*, (London: Thames & Hudson, 2003)

[2] Romans 8:31.

14

Why Is This Night Different?

The Passover is the greatest single event in Hebrew history. Nothing measures up to it—not the calling of Abraham, Moses receiving the Torah, or the founding of David's kingdom compares to it. It was the pivotal point when they became God's firstborn. The Passover should be seen as second only to the Resurrection as the greatest moment in the Christian faith. It foretold the Savior's sacrifice to come.

Most of the points made in this chapter come from Ceil and Moishe Rosen's outstanding book, *Christ in the Passover*. I would be doing a great disservice to try to regurgitate it here in these few pages. However, some of those points have to be reviewed for completeness.

The word "phrasal," or Passover, is unusual in that, like the name Moses, it is actually an ancient Egyptian word that was incorporated into the Hebrew. When people hear the term, most think of God overlooking sin or passing on the judgment resulting from sin. But the English translation of Passover really misses the true implications of the word. The literal definition of the word is "to spread the wings over"—as in protecting. This gives the Savior's lament new context when he wept over Jerusalem and said, "Oh Jerusalem, Jerusalem … how I wish to protect you as a hen protects her chicks."[1]

The main elements of Passover listed in Exodus are bitter herbs, unleavened bread, lamb, and lamb's blood. Considering each of these will help in appreciating the deeper meaning of Passover.

Jews, by tradition, consider the bitter herbs as a symbol of the bitterness of oppressive bondage under the Egyptians. To this day, they will dip lettuce leaves in salt water as part of the Passover meal and view the salt water as representing the tears their ancestors shed as slaves. Christians can see how these same bitter herbs point to the bitterness of the oppression of sin and to the tears of the desperate sinner seeking salvation.

Leaven (with the one exception of Jesus' parable[2]) is symbolic of sin. It's obvious that the removal of yeast from the Israelite's houses[3] shows the need of removing sin from their lives. Passover is the beginning of the Feast of Unleavened Bread, in which for seven days the Hebrews eat nothing with yeast. It is a purification of sin that coincides with the creation cycle of seven days. In a way, the Israelites became new, sinless creatures.

The lamb should be obvious, especially bearing in mind John the Baptist calling Jesus "the Lamb of God who will take the sin from the world".[4] Some think this reference is to the sin sacrifice of the Mosaic Law, but it's really an allusion to Passover. Consider that God directs the Israelite's not to break the lambs' bones,[5] and compare that to the fulfilled prophecy in which none of Jesus' bones were broken on the cross.[6]

The emblem of Christ as the Passover Lamb is strengthened by the fact that the Passover lambs (and all lambs for sacrifice) were to be without blemish or spot. They were physically what Jesus was spiritually. And the lambs were to be roasted only over an open flame, as if they were a sacrifice. Recall how Paul admonishes the Corinthians not to participate in pagan sacrifices.[7] That reprimand might seem strange because earlier in the letter, he spoke of food being sacrificed to idols as nothing. But he is making an important distinction. Partaking in the ritual and in eating the sacrifice sanctifies a person. This is what was so radical about Jesus instituting the Lord's Supper, or the Eucharist. By tradition, the last thing to be eaten in the Passover meal was the lamb. When at the end of the Last Supper Jesus took the bread and said, "This is my body," He was, in effect, saying He was the Passover Lamb. Paul confirms this statement was our Lord's intended meaning in a letter to the Corinthians.[8]

Moreover, the "sprinkling" of the lamb's blood on the lintel and post of the door points to the Lord's crucifixion. The Israelites collected the blood in a basin,[9] but the term suggests the gutter at the doorstep of the house. And the "sprinkling" really means to brush or to paint the doorframe. Essentially, the Israelites were passing through the lamb's blood to obtain salvation. Perhaps our Lord was alluding to this incident when He said, "I am the door and whoever enters through me will be saved."[10]

Consider all of the parts of Passover together, and see how what Israel did in the flesh the church does in the spirit. They passed through the blood of a sacrifice to gain salvation and were sanctified by partaking in the perfect sacrifice that drives out sin and makes them new creations removed from the bitterness of bondage.

Chapter 14 Endnotes

[1] Luke 13:34.
[2] Matthew 13:33.
[3] Exodus 12:15.
[4] John 1:29 and Psalms 34:20.
[5] Exodus 12:46 and Numbers 9:12
[6] John 19:36
[7] I Corinthians 10:18-20
[8] I Corinthians 5:7
[9] Exodus 12:22
[10] John 10:9

15

The First Harvest

The Law, the Convent, the Teaching, the Torah; this was God's special gift to the Israelites through Moses. It is a gift that sanctified Israel, set her apart from the world, and made her a nation of priest, whose mission was to teach the world the true righteousness of the one true God.[1] Its application, structure, presentation, and timing, disclose not only God's master plan, but also His willingness to compensate for man's frailty. Moreover, it shows the greatness of the Torah.

Many people say that there is nothing new in the Torah. All of the great civilizations had moral and ethical codes. All of them had a respect for the divine and strict rules of conduct that, if not always held in practice, were at least esteemed in the ideal. In some ways, those critics are correct, and Christians should have no problem in acknowledging that point. After all, the Apostle Paul stated that God had written the Torah on the hearts of men.[2] C. S. Lewis illustrated this fully when he took the ethical writings throughout the world and history and then laid them out in what he called the Toa. He showed that every culture held moral prohibitions against murder and defrauding fellow tribesmen, and all esteemed honesty. Some concept of the divine held sway in all of those cultures (true, most were intolerant toward views of the divine not their own).[3] This tendency in humanity is so universal that many behavioralists and anthropologists deem it as something evolving to increase survival of the species. This is odd, particularly when Victor Frankl's experience in the Nazi concentration camps showed that strictly following moral codes actually limits an individual's chances of survival and, therefore, the species. In his own words,

> On the average, only those prisoners could keep alive who, after years of trekking from camp to camp, had lost all scruples in their fight for existence; they were prepared

to use every means, honest and otherwise, even brutal force, theft, and betrayal of their friends, in order to save themselves. We who have come back ... know: the best of us did not return.[4]

Although the substance of the Law is analogous to other ethical codes, it is unique in its application. Where as other codes of conduct were binding only between members of the same tribe, the Torah required the Israelites to treat the foreigner with the same justice they treated one another.[5] Moreover, they were commanded to love the alien,[6] even the Egyptians who had enslaved them.[7] The rules of ethics were to be applied equally to all in the society—the widow, the poor, the stranger—and even the slave. The law had several lengthy passages on the treatment of slaves and how even minor mistreatments resulted in their being set free.[8] An Israelite could not be in good standing with God if he failed to treat his servant and the alien with the same respect he treated his brother. This just and merciful treatment of the most vulnerable is what made the Torah exceptional in ancient—and even modern—times.

Not only was the application unique but also elements of its very structure were exceptional. The first three commandments deal with man's relationship to God and how to venerate Him. The last six direct man's conduct toward his fellow man. The fourth commandment, the day of rest, was exceptional. No other moral code required the suspension of work and activity. At first, this commandment is mystifying, but after consideration, it becomes obvious why this commandment is there and was so fervently enforced. Ethical codes can easily be intellectualized, but it takes constant reflection to internalize them. One day out of seven without the distractions of daily living forces contemplation on the Lord God and His teachings. It is a meditation that compels ethics to seep into the heart and not to only remain in the mind.

The almost Hollywood production of giving the Torah may explain why God chooses to speak to men in that "still small voice" He spoke to Elijah.[9] After all, the people begged Moses to relay the teaching to them because the power and majesty of God were more than they could withstand.[10] Even with this mighty display, they chose to ignore God. A mere forty days later, they were worshiping an idol and ready to return to slavery. It shows that powerful and miraculous signs have, at best, a short-term effect on those who's hearts are not ready to bend to God. But those who are ready only need a "still small voice." That readiness comes with time. We must remember that Moses' father-in-law was a priest of the Most High God. Maybe those forty years of shepherding flocks and being with Jethro were the preparation Moses required to stand before the burning bush.

Thomas Cahill points out that the Lord had to take the Israelites into the wilderness to strip away their old lives to make them a new people.[11] The Torah would never have taken root if it had been given in Egypt or Canaan. The temptations and sensual rituals would've overwhelmed it. The Israelites were not yet a distinct people. Four hundred years of Egyptian influence had made them more Egyptian than Semitic, and without a proper rooting in the teaching, they would've become Canaanites. As it was, forty years of indoctrination and wiping out an entire generation were not enough It finally took the scourge of captivity and the lost of the homeland to keep them faithful.

Along with God's staging, there is His timing. Recall that the Passover lamb was killed on the fourteenth day of the first month,[12] and the Israelites came to the mountain on the first day of the third month.[13] Add to that the day Moses brought the elders to the mountain and the three days of purification. You now have fifty days since the Passover, or a Pentecost. The Feast of Weeks was also known as the Feast of Harvest, which is very telling. There is great symmetry in having the day the Law was given coincide with the day the Church began. But what's even more telling is the consequence of each. The Israelites in the desert became impatient with "Moses tarrying on the mountain" and rejected the true God for an idol. The result was that 3,000 were slain for their sins.[14] While at Pentecost, the Jews embraced the Messiah, and 3,000 souls were added to the kingdom.[15] The Torah and the Church both give righteousness to man. The Torah shows the exacting justice of God, and its rejection brought death at its very founding. The Church, however, exhibits God's loving mercy, and its acceptance ushered in salvation from the beginning. The final irony was that it was at the harvest. Jesus was pointing to this day when He said that "the fields are white for the harvest."[16] At Sinai was a harvest of justice, at Pentecost a harvest of mercy, and each in equal measure.

Chapter 15 Endnotes

[1] Exodus 19:6.
[2] Romans 2:14–15.
[3] C. S. Lewis, *The Abolition of Man* (New York: Simon & Schuster, 1944), appendix, "Illustrations of the Toa."
[4] Victor E. Frankl, *Man's Search for Meaning* (New York: Pocket Books, 1971, original 1959), p. 7.
[5] Deuteronomy 27:19.
[6] Leviticus 19:34 and Deuteronomy 10:18–19.
[7] Deuteronomy 23:7.
[8] Exodus 21.
[9] I Kings 19:12.
[10] Exodus 20:19.
[11] Thomas Cahill, *The Gift of the Jews: How a Tribe of Desert Nomads Changed the Way Everyone Thinks and Feels* (New York: Doubleday, 1998), p. 160
[12] Exodus 12:6.
[13] Exodus 20:1.
[14] Exodus 32:28.
[15] Acts 2:41.
[16] John 4:35.

16

The Tabernacle

The Law that Moses brought down from the Mountain of the Lord was more than a moral code and dietary directions, which receives most of the attention. It had another component, one that is in some ways the most important. It gave direction on the elements of worship. The first of which was the Tabernacle.[1]

The Tabernacle should echo in the Christian mind: the colors involved, the articles placed in it, and even its layout. The number three constantly appears. There were three areas: the courtyard, the Holy Place, and the Holy of Holies. There were three colors: blue, purple, and scarlet. (Remember, these colors weren't just colors but royal colors.) There were three articles in the Holy Place, and three items in the Ark of the Covenant. Threes upon threes upon threes should scream out the very essence of the Almighty to the Christian—and the Tabernacle emphasized it. A deeper look will show even more symbolism.

Let's start with courtyard. At the entrance is the Brazen Altar, and immediately following it is the bronze Laver. To gain admission to the House of God, people had to offer a sacrifice and take a purified washing—just as admittance into the Church requires Christ's sacrifice and baptism.

Once sanctified by sacrifice and washed clean of impurity, the priest could enter the Holy Place, where three pieces of furniture resided. The first was the lamp stand giving light to the dark sanctuary. The lamp had a total of seven lights, which symbolized the seven days of the week or the seven days of the creation cycle. Just as God said, "Let there be light," in the dark universe, He also illuminates the human heart. And true enlightenment is a daily thing. Just as the lamp must be continually lit, man must maintain God's light within. The second was the table of Show Bread, which had twelve unleavened cakes. The cakes are sinless bread that sustains and sanctifies the priest in his duties while wondering in the Desert of Sin.[2] In like fashion, Jesus, the bread of life,[3] sustains the Christian in his sojourn through a sinful world. The final item was the Altar of Incense, which stood before the entry of the Holy of Holies. Incense has often been a symbol of prayer rising to Heaven.[4] This altar pointed to the Holy Spirit as He "intercedes for us with groans that words cannot express"[5] to the Father. Then there's the veil leading to the Most Holy Place.

Crossing the veil, there was a perfect cube of ten cubits by ten cubits by ten cubits at the center of the Tabernacle. For pagan temples, the innermost sanctum was the location of the deity or at least its image. But God had forbidden any graven image; besides, how could human hands carve anything that could represent God. Spirit cannot be shown in the physical realm. All that can be shown is the effect of spirit; even then the artificial will be sorely lacking. The only things that can represent God are the things that are themselves from God. So it was with the Tabernacle.

At the center of the Holy of Holies were three special objects. The first, the stone tablets with the Law that was designed to make man Holy and written by the finger of God—an everlasting law shattered by man. Second, manna, bread from heaven that gave life to the Israelites. And finally, the rod of Aaron, the dead stick brought back to life so fully that it blossomed with almond buds. A collection of three items that should be unsurprising to the Christian, after all, we do accept the Trinity of Father, Son, and Holy Spirit. The shattered tablets of the covenant can be seen as the Father, because they were the statutes that bound Israel—"God's firstborn"[6]—to God. The jar of manna is obviously the Lord Jesus. He refers to Himself as the "bread of life,"[7] and He, like it, came down from heaven. The rod of Aaron, a dead stick of wood made alive, shows that Aaron and Moses held God's favor and selection of priesthood. In like manner, the Holy Spirit dwells in the Christian heart, which was once dead in sin and is now spiritually alive. Three separate items bound together in the Ark of the Covenant, just as God is three but one.

The Mercy Seat of the Ark was where the Glory of God resided, and the veil was always between God and His people. Before the Tabernacle could be dismantled and moved, the veil was taken down and covered the Ark.[8] It was as if the Most Holy Place was collapsed on to the Ark ; forming an impenetrable separation between God and His people, except for once a year when the High Priest brought the blood of atonement. And so it was until the Great High Priest[9] entered with blood from a sacrifice sufficient to atone for all time, and then the veil was torn by God.

This veil was made of all three colors in the Tabernacle: blue, purple, and scarlet.[10] Moreover, blue is the color for heaven, purple is the color for kings, and scarlet is the color of blood. (What's even more telling is that scarlet yarn was used in the cleansing from disease ceremony.[11] It points to the idea of Christ's blood cleansing the sinner and breaking his bonds.) These three colors were interwoven to make the veil that separated the Ark in the Holy of Holies. When transporting the Tabernacle, all of the sacred articles were covered with blue cloth except for two. The Show Bread Table was covered with a scarlet cloth and the Altar with a purple one.[12] To the Christian, these actions point to Jesus: with the scarlet pointing to His sacrifice and the purple showing it to be a kingly sacrifice to the Father.

To comprehend the final component of the Tabernacle, one must understand the ancient view toward temples and recall that the Israelites had just escaped Egypt. Their view of the spiritual realm would be greatly influenced by their 400 years in Egypt. Temples were not considered in the same way as churches and synagogues are today. Temples were not figurative "houses of God" where people congregate to gain a spiritual connection to the infinite God, to learn of Him, or to discuss His commands; those concepts didn't come about until the Babylonian captivity. To the ancients, a temple was the literal house of a god. In the inner sanctuary was the location of the idol that would be brought out only on special occasions, if at all. After conquering Jerusalem, the Roman general, Pompey, entered the Holy of Holies in hopes of seeing what the Hebrew God looked like and was shocked to find the place empty.[13]

God knew that the Israelites were not emotionally, intellectually, or spiritually ready to make a radical break from all they understood. Hence, the reason He chose to model the Tabernacle after the gentile temples. It was to be a dwelling for Him to be among His people. This is why His glory rested over the Most Holy place.[14]

However, one radical difference existed between the Tabernacle and the Egyptian temples. In Egypt, the people resided, held commerce, and completed all the other actions of their daily lives on one side of the Nile, while the temples of the gods were on the other side. Although they held allegiance to their gods and held festivals in their honor, there was still a separation. With the Israelites, the Tabernacle was placed in the center of the camp with three tribes on each side of it. God was in the very center of their lives and dwelled in their midst. He was not like the gods of Egypt who were far away and could be appeased by a few rituals made by a priest. With the Hebrews, the Lord was always present and everyday required commitment to Him. The Tabernacle was the focal point of the Israelites community and their lives, just as God is at the center (or should be) of the Christian heart.

Chapter 16 Endnotes

[1] Exodus 25:10–27:19.
[2] Exodus 16:1
[3] John 6:35.
[4] Psalms 141:2.
[5] Romans 8:26.
[6] Exodus 4:22.
[7] John 6:35.
[8] Numbers 4:5.
[9] Hebrews 4;14.
[10] Exodus 25:4.
[11] Leviticus 14:4.
[12] Numbers 4:1–15.
[13] Flavius Josephus, *Antiquitates Judaicae*, book 14, chapter 4.
[14] Exodus 40:34–35.

17

The Priest

The priest is the liaison from man to God just as the prophet is God's link to man. Both offices are filled by God's choice and not man's. Under the Torah, it was by birth in the Aaronic bloodline. In the Messianic age, it is also by birth or, more accurately, rebirth of the Christian. In both dispensations, God chose the priest. In both cases, a priest was purified and consecrated through sacrifice[1]

After bringing a bull, two rams, and a basket of unleavened cakes before for the Lord, Moses washed and anointed Aaron and his sons. They were then consecrated through sacrifice.

The bull was a sin offering that cleansed the priest's souls, and the first ram, along with some of the unleavened bread, were a burnt offering given completely to God. The second ram was an offering that consecrated the priest. The blood of this offering mixed with anointing oil was sprinkled on the priest. The portions of the sacrifice were waved before God, and the priest then feasted on it and the unleavened cakes. This sacrifice was placed on the priest both outside and the inside so that it completely permeated his body. It was this sacrifice before God that made the priest holy and purified him to perform his duties before God. By eating the sacrifice to God, it bound his soul to God, and therefore, the leftover could not be eaten by anyone else and had to be burned.

Considering this ritual, one can understand why the Jews were so opposed to eating meat offered to an idol. Although Paul said that an idol was nothing, he did admit that participating in the pagan festivals was unprofitable and was like feasting at the table of demons. As he said, "you cannot take of the cup of the Lord and then take of the cup of demons."[2]

In like fashion, Christ's sacrifice consecrates the Christian. Like Aaron and his sons, we show our willingness to be cleansed through a washing. They were anointed with oil and the ram's blood. We are anointed with the Holy Spirit and the blood of our Redeemer. Their sanctification was made complete by eating the sacrifice. So to is the Christian who eats the sacrifice made to God. He eats the body of Christ and drinks His blood so that Christ's sacrifice completely permeates his existence.

One more thing seems unusual in the ceremony. Some of the blood from the offering was placed on the right earlobe, right thumb, and the right big toe.[3] It seems completely out of place, but when you consider the office of priest it may not seem so strange. He officiates the worship of God, but he is also to present God's commandments to God's people. This is especially important for the Hebrews because they were to be "a race of priest." Their mission was to present God to the world; a charge that still befalls Israel, even under the Messianic age and under the Melchizedekian priesthood. Exactly how is this responsibility enacted? This ceremony is the perfect symbolism of how it is done. You must first hear the commands of God; thus, the earlobe. Then you have to act on those commands because just hearing is not enough; thus, the blood on the thumb. Finally, to fulfill the office of priest, you have to take what you heard to the world; thus, the blood on the big toe. All three facets of the priestly office are reiterated in the New Testament. Paul points out that "faith comes from hearing";[4] James asserted that "I will show you my faith by what I do";[5] and Paul quoted Isaiah saying "how beautiful are the feet of those who brings the gospel."[6] If that is not enough, our Lord Himself summed the priestly responsibility with the last words He spoke on this earth when He proclaimed, "go and make disciples of all nations ... teaching them to obey everything I have commanded you."[7]

Chapter 17 Endnotes

[1] Exodus 29 and Leviticus 8 (each entire chapter covers the ordainment of the priest).
[2] I Corinthians 10:21.
[3] Exodus 29:20 and Leviticus 8:24.
[4] Romans 10:17.
[5] James 2:18.
[6] Romans 10:15 and Isaiah 52:7.
[7] Matthew 28:19–20.

18

Sacrifices

There were five types of sacrifices or offerings listed in the Torah: sin, trespass, fellowship, grain, and burnt. Each of the sacrifices has a correlation in Christianity.

The sin offering is obviously Christ's sacrifice on the cross. It was given for inadvertent and unknowing sins committed against God. Sins of open defiance were punishable by death. This shows how much greater Christ's sacrifice was, because it can also wipe away the stain of rebellion. There are some other things about the sin offering that really points to Christ. It was a sacrifice given when a leper came before the priest to be cleansed.[1] And just as when the priests were sanctified; some blood of the offering was placed on the earlobe, the thumb and the big toe of the cleansed man. Leprosy is often symbolic of sin, and how better to declare cleansing of body and soul than through the sin sacrifice? Christ did the same with His sacrifice. It should also be noted that when the sin offering was given for the whole nation, the high priest took the blood and sprinkle it before the veil that separated the Holy of Holies from the Holy Place.[2] When Christ died, God Himself tore the veil in half from top to bottom. This tearing symbolized man's free access to his creator. It is an access made possible by the ultimate sin offering that had been sprinkled before the true veil separating the true Holy of Holies in heaven.

The guilt or trespass offering would also seem to be covered by the cross. But it represents another area in the Christian life. The primary difference between this offering and that of sin was the injured party. The sin offering was solely to make man right with God, but the trespass offering covered actions done against a brother. The law required not only compensation in excess as a penalty,[3] but it also required a sacrifice. Christianity also calls for a sacrifice, but with a difference. Recall what is said in the Lord's Prayer, "forgive us our trespasses as we forgive those who trespass against us."[4] And recollect Jesus' answer to Peter's question of how often we must forgive our brothers, "not seven times but seventy times seven."[5] Also bear in mind the direction given at the Sermon on the Mount: we are to pray for those who harm us and to bless those who hate us.[6] Where the Torah called for the offender to give a sacrifice, Christianity has the offended sacrificing. The Christian forgoes his right of retribution and more. He must also forgive and pray for the one who committed the crime against him.

Under the Torah, the peace or fellowship offering was optional, whereas in Christianity it is almost commanded. This sacrifice was offered in three situations and was often given different names. The first was giving thanks for unmerited or unexpected blessings and was called a praise offering.[7] If it was also made at the completion of a vow.[8] And finally, if it was made out of love for God, it was called a freewill offering.[9] What made it unique was that friends and family were called to share in the offering and a feast usually accompanied the sacrifice.[10] For Christians, this offering is made through the assembly of the saints[11] and the love feast with one another.[12] In our coming together, we express the joy of peace and fellowship with one another, and we use our freewill to express our love for our Lord by constantly renewing our vow to follow Him; praising Him for the unmerited blessing of grace.

The grain offering is once again one of those in which the correlation in Christianity should be obvious. It was the fruits of man's own effort and hard work, and by giving the first fruits, man showed his faith that God would provide for him.[13] Giving is the grain offering for the Christian, and it is necessary, but not to supply the church's needs. God is all powerful—He will meet all the requirements. No, the necessity of the Christian's giving is to break mammon's hold. Bear in mind, the grain offering was never given by itself, it was always given in conjunction with either the peace (fellowship) offering or a burnt sacrifice.[14] Just giving money is never enough; the Macedonians' giving was greater because they first gave themselves.[15]

The burnt sacrifice was unique in that no portion of it was ever given to the priest. It was an offering given totally to God. Every bit was burned and nothing was left.[16] Moreover, the Israelites were directed to give a burnt offering in the morning and evening so as to be an unceasing sacrifice of devotion to God.[17] However, things that were not normally sacrifices could be given "as a burnt offering." This is not to say they were laid on the altar and burned. Jephthah's daughter was given as a burnt sacrifice, which meant that her entire life was given over to God.[18] She never married and probably lived in the Tabernacle performing services for the priest and Levis, such as by cooking or cleaning. Similarly, Hannah gave Samuel to Eli's care after he was weaned, and his life was in total dedication to God.[19] Christians are called to be "living sacrifices" for God.[20] Everything the Christian is and everything he does goes to the glory of God. Our lives are no longer our own; we have been sacrificed so that we "no longer live, but Christ lives in [us]."[21] In short, we are the burnt offerings to God.

Chapter 18 Endnotes

[1] Leviticus 14 12–18.
[2] Leviticus 4: 13–21.
[3] Leviticus 6:5–6.
[4] Matthew 6:12.
[5] Matthew 18:22.
[6] Matthew 5:44.
[7] Leviticus 7:12–15.
[8] Leviticus 7:16
[9] Leviticus 7:28-34.
[10] Deuteronomy 12:6–7 and 17–18.
[11] Hebrews 10:25.
[12] Jude 1:12.
[13] Leviticus 2:14.
[14] Numbers 15:1–13.
[15] II Corinthians 8:1–5.
[16] Leviticus 1:5–17 and 6:8–13.
[17] Exodus 29:38–42 and Numbers 28:3–8.
[18] Judges 11:30–38.
[19] I Samuel 1:22.
[20] Romans 12:1.
[21] Galatians 2:20.

19

Elements of Worship

Let us review the last three chapters and consider the implications. God gave the Israelites elements necessary and sufficient for worship. By this, I mean that if you have those ingredients, you have worship; if you are to worship, you must have those components.

The first of the components was the Temple, or in the Israelites' case, the Tabernacle. However, the Tabernacle was nothing more than a mobile temple of cloth, and the Temple was a fixed tabernacle of stone. The Christian has a new Temple—a temple of flesh. For our bodies are God's temple,[1] and we are the "living stones" of a greater temple.[2] Just as God's Glory hovered over the Tabernacle[3] and completely filled the Temple at its dedication,[4] so the Holy Spirit resides in our hearts and His glory shines out through our good deeds.

The second is the priesthood, which was ordained and made sinless by the partaking of a sacrifice. So the Christian is part of a holy nation of priest[5] ordained by the sacrifice of Jesus and made pure by the taking of the Lord's Supper (or Eucharist). Moreover, our high priest brings the blood of atonement before God, not one day of the year, but continually so that our purity is everlasting.[6]

The third is the sacrifice, specifically, the burnt offering. It was a sacrifice that was totally given to God and not one part held back for the priest or the one offering it. It was a sacrifice that was given in the morning and the evening; in other words, it was constantly offered. The Christian's very life is given as a burnt offering because we are to be living sacrifices.[7]

So the three parts of worship are the temple, priest, and sacrifice. These are always with a Christian. To worship, you must have these things, and to have them, means to worship. The implication should be terrifying. Worship is more then meeting on Sunday, reading the Bible, or praying. Since the elements of worship are always with a Christian, then a Christian is always in worship. The Christian life is nothing but worship. That means to fail to do your best in anything should be an anathema, because you are failing to worship God properly. It would be the same as placing a lame or blemished lamb on the altar, which was an offense worthy of Divine wrath.

Chapter 19 Endnotes

[1] I Corinthians 10:19.
[2] 1 Peter 2:5.
[3] Numbers 9:15–23.
[4] II Chronicles 5:14.
[5] I Peter 2:9.
[6] Hebrews 9:24–26.
[7] Romans 12:1.

20

The Feasts

Passover, the Feast of Weeks, and the Feast of the Tabernacles are the three great feasts passed down from Moses. All of them have their corresponding point in Christianity.

Passover celebrates the events of Exodus, where the Israelites were freed from bondage by God's power. Every year, Jews hold a Seder to commemorate those events and to remind themselves that they are a special people only because God chose them. If not for the grace of God, the blood of the lamb would never have stayed the hand of the Angel of Death. Christians also have a Seder to honor God's breaking of their bondage, and they know that but for the grace of God they would be condemned to death under the slavery of sin. Christians call the Seder by different names: Catholics call it the Eucharist, Protestants refer to it as the Holy Communion, and the Bible identifies it as the Lord's Supper. Where the Jews observe their Seder annually, Christians celebrate theirs weekly. Each recognize the sacrificial lamb that saves them from death, for the Christian that lamb was the Messiah.

The Feast of Weeks was also the feast of the harvest. As was mentioned earlier, this feast also coincided with the presentation of the Torah to the Israelites. But it also matches with the Christian Pentecost. In the Feast of Weeks, the Jews received the Law that consecrated them, while the church received the Holy Spirit who sanctifies them. In the first, justice caused the death of 3,000 while the grace of the second brought new life to 3,000. Both are a celebration of harvesting. The first is the physical harvest that ensured another year of life, while the other is a spiritual harvest that guarantees eternal life, and with "the fields white already to harvest,"[198] it sent the workers out in the field.

With the Passover corresponding to the crucifixion and the Feast of Weeks corresponding to the Pentecost, then the Feast of the Tabernacles should relate to something with the New Covenant, but what? Nothing in the Gospels or Acts really jumps out, but it seems that something should.

Consider the activities of the feast that go on to this day in the Jewish community (particularly the Orthodox communities). First, Jews spend a week outdoors in booths they construct to remind them of the wandering in the wilderness.[199] Then on the eighth day, they have a riotous celebration that could rival Fat Tuesday of Mardi Gras. A. J. Jacobs, in his book *The Year of Living Biblically*, told how strange it was to see Hasidic Jews, who were normally so solemn and dignified, laughing, joking, drinking, and dancing with such abandonment.[200] As mentioned, their festivities could rival Fat Tuesday, but with one big difference. Fat Tuesday is a final blowout before Lent. It is a perversion, because it is seen as the last chance to have fun before a forced penance. However, the Jewish holiday comes out of the joy of goodness and thanksgiving that springs from the favor of God. The emphasis is so much better and so much purer—it is a joy of coming into the Promise Land after the sorrows of wandering in the wilderness. Remember that it is also called the Feast of Ingathering, and it was a celebration of the end of the harvest. It's the last of the three annual feasts.

If you think in spiritual terms, then the Feast of Tabernacles should be obvious. Christians today are living in the temporal booths of their earthly bodies; they are wandering in the sinful wilderness of this world. We too will someday have a final ingathering that brings us into a promised land. When that happens, there will be such an outpouring of thankfulness that our joy will cause us to dance before the Lord with laughter.

The Passover was the crucifixion; the Feast of Weeks was the Pentecost; and the Feast of Tabernacles will be the second coming. Only the Father knows the exact day and the exact hour,[201] but I think I may know which day of the year it will be.

Chapter 20 Endnotes

[1] John 4:35
[2] Leviticus 23:39–43.
[3] A. J. Jacobs, *The Year of Living Biblically* (New York: Simon & Schuster, 2007), pp. 84–87.
[4] Matthew 24:36.

21

Temptations

One of the most consistent themes of the wilderness wandering is Israel's constant temptation to sin and their failure in resisting it.

From the very beginning, Israel doubted God's power to care for them. The Israelites' amnesia of the plagues in Egypt and the destruction of Pharaoh's chariots in the Red Sea[1] is bewildering. You would think they could see a God powerful enough to do all of that is one who could care for them in the desert. Still, they grumbled about the lack of drinkable water at Marah,[2] about the lack of water at Massah,[3] and finally the lack of food.[4] However, God was very patient with them. He understood their concerns and was willing to be tolerant. However His forbearance did have its limits, and it was reached when they worshiped the Golden Calf.[5] From that point onward, their grumblings are followed by the phrase, "God's anger burned against them."[6]

This anger is seen when the Israelites complained about the manna and wanted meat. God was so angry that He sent them quail, and more quail, and more quail. He sent them so much quail to the point that they got sick of it and it came out of their nostrils. But when the Israelites forgot to thank Him, God struck them with a plague "while the meat was still in their teeth."[7]

The Israelites succumbed to grumbling again on the plains of Moab, and they whined that they should have died in Egypt or in the desert rather than by the sword to foreign soldiers. And for good measure, they added to the list about how tired they were of the food. God was more than willing to oblige and sent fiery snakes. Many died until Moses raised the bronze serpent.[8] And still they grumbled. Over and over and over again they were unthankful to God and forgot how many times He had provided for them. Their unjustified lack of faith and trust was their undoing.

If ingratitude and grumbling were not enough, Israel also provoked God's jealousy. First with the Golden Calf and then with the Midianites, they played the harlot—quite literally—with other gods.[9] The euphemism, "they got up to play," meant they had an orgy. Many of the Middle Eastern gods were fertility gods, and sex was one of the offerings of worship. The need to divorce the Israelites from such debauchery could explain why God was so adamant that the priests never show their nakedness before the altar.[9] Ba'al of Peor was probably a fertility god. The action of Phinehas against Zimri and Cozbi suggest this.[11] Israel's desire to be like the other nations and have other gods along with God caused the greatest punishments. It is at those points that the Bible tells of thousands of Israelites dying from God's anger.

God's rage was also kindled at the continual refusal to accept Moses' authority as His agent. There was the outright rebellion of the 250 Levis led by Korah and Kohath who desired to take the priesthood from Aaron.[12] It was resolved by the contest of the firepans, and the fire from the glory of God consumed the 250 offering the incense. Of course, this uprising was a double revolt with Dathan and Aribam from the tribe of Ruben contesting Moses' political leadership.[13] With them, God stepped in once again, and the earth swallowed them and everyone in their households. Even with this display of divine appointment, the people still grumbled and blamed Moses for the rebels' deaths. Once again, the Lord had to rebuke, and 14,700 died of plague.[14] Even then, the Israelites wouldn't accept this judgment until God gave the sign of Aaron's staff budding.[15]

Moses' own family opposed him, when Miriam and Aaron took offense at his marriage to a Cushite woman. They both went before the people and asked, "Does God speak only to Moses?"[16] God rebuked them and struck Miriam with leprosy as punishment for her conceit.

Looking at the Israelites' temptations, you can see that they fall into three areas: their physical needs, such as food and water; their desire to be like the other nations by worshiping additional gods; and their requiring proof of Moses' relationship with God. And these temptations are the very same ones the Messiah experienced in His ministry.[17] First, in the desert after fasting for forty days, He was tempted to change stones into bread—just as the Hebrews were tempted to worry about physical needs rather than trust in God's ability to provide. Second, He was offered the whole world if He would worship the tempter—just as the Israelites wanted to have influence in the world by assimilating their neighbors' customs and gods. Finally, He was challenged to prove His divine standing by casting himself from the temple to show the miracle of His angelic salvation—just as the Israelites demanded signs that God was with Moses. In each case, Jesus remained sinless. But these were not the only times He was tempted. The people came to Him during His ministry and suggested He feed them when they said, "Our forefathers ate manna in the wilderness."[18] Again He refused. And there was the time of the triumphal entry into Jerusalem when the people called for Him to be king,[19] and His disciples begged Him to restore Judah to the glory of Solomon.[20] But He rejected the false god of political empire. Time and time again, the scribes and Pharisees called for confirmation of His authority to teach and for signs of His relationship with God—they even called for it while He was dying on the cross.[21] Every time He declined.

The poor wanted Jesus to be a peoples' Messiah who would rescue them for their plight and ensure that their physical needs were met. It was the same type of grumbling as "what shall we eat and what shall we drink." The Zealots wanted a kingly Messiah who would liberate them from Rome and return Judea to a glorious golden age. They wanted an icon of power that would give them influence among their neighbor nations. The Pharisees wanted a miraculous Messiah who would demonstrate His divine dominance.

The problem was that the Jews hadn't changed since their time in the desert, for those desires were the same ones the Israelites showed to Moses. Unfortunately, these tendencies are the same in today's Christians. The popularity of the prosperity gospel, as typified by the *Prayer of Jabez*, is our wish to increase our physical domain rather than deepen our spiritual understanding of the Word of God. The expansion of the charismatic branches of all denominations shows our desire to put God to the test by placing our hope in signs of faith over the more excellent way of love. Finally, our uniting under political action committees and following liberation theology are nothing more than falling down to the idol of cultural influence and trying to be like the other nations instead of picking up our cross to serve God in true discipleship.

The saddest thing of all is that this is an eternal fight. The Hebrews fought this issue throughout their history, and sadder still is that Christians with the full explanation of the old and new covenant are fighting it too.

Paul warns the Corinthians in placing too high of a premium on outward signs,[22] and Peter warns against false teachers.[23] Worse still, it has been a core theme in Christian history. Dostoevsky gives an unsettling review of Christianity's yielding to these temptations with his parable of the Inquisitor.[24] And this shows that people of faith will constantly fight and often yield to those temptations for all time. We are the children of Eve's deception. We still see the fruit as "good for food, a delight to the eyes, and desirable to make one wise."[25] That is why we need salvation because we always seek "what we will eat and what we will wear,"[26] before the kingdom of God. We will want to walk by the sight of miracles and signs rather than by faith. And we will forever ask the Messiah at the end of His ministry if now He will restore Israel to its glory.[27]

The Bronze Serpent

Why in the world did God have Moses make the bronze serpent? It seems so out of place, and it even appears to violate His own prohibition against graven images. In fact, the next time it's mentioned is when King Hezekiah had to destroy it because the Jews were worshiping it by burning incense to it.[28] And it's even more surprising considering what happened to Eve in the garden. It seems so strange that God would command this. Here was a symbol of the very thing inflicting so much pain to His people; moreover, it was an accursed symbol. But it was pointing to something greater. The third, and final time, the bronze serpent is mentioned in the Bible is by the Messiah when Nicodemus came to Him at night. The Lord said, "Like the serpent was raised in the desert, so must the Son of Man be raised up."[29] Just as Israel looked up to an accursed symbol to be saved from death by the bite of the fiery snakes, so to does the Christian look to the accursed cross (for "anyone who is hung on a tree is accursed of God")[30] to be saved from death by the fiery bite of sin. Just as later generations of Jews looked to this symbol with affection and worship in memory of how it saved them, so too does the Christian look upon the cross. And the Christian of today must not make the mistake the Jews of King Hezekiah's time made by worshiping the symbol and not the God who is the power behind it.

Chapter 21 Endnotes

[1] Exodus 14:28.
[2] Exodus 15:23–25.
[3] Exodus 17:1–6.
[4] Exodus 16:1–4.
[5] Exodus 32.
[6] Exodus 32; Numbers 11, 12, 14, and 32.
[7] Number 11:20–35.
[8] Numbers 21.
[9] Numbers 25.
[10] Exodus 20:26.
[11] Numbers 25:8.
[12] Numbers 16
[13] Numbers 16
[14] Numbers 16
[15] Numbers 17
[16] Numbers 12:1
[17] Matthew 4 and Luke 4.
[18] John 6:30.
[19] Matthew 21:1–11; Mark 11:1–11; Luke 19:18–41; and John 12:12–16.
[20] Acts 1:6.
[21] Matthew 27:40 and Mark 15:32.
[22] I Corinthians 12.
[23] II Peter 2:1.
[24] Fyodor Dostoevsky, *The Brothers Karamazov* (Lyndhurst, NJ: Barnes and Noble Classics, 1994), book 5, chapter 5.
[25] Genesis 3:6
[26] Matthew 6:31
[27] Acts 1:6
[28] II Kings 18:4
[29] John 3:14.
[30] Deuteronomy 21:23.

22
Balaam

Why was God angry at Balaam for going with Barak's emissaries after He gave permission to go? The fact that He said "no" and then said "you may" is very confusing and controversial.[1] In many ways, it is such a bizarre tale that some theologians think is satire about the unnatural perversions of the pagan prophets. Bible skeptics point to it as "proof" of God's capacious nature. And the first part of Balaam's story is a difficult passage to comprehend.

For the Christian, I think the key is what Paul told the Corinthians when he said, "all things are lawful, but not all things edify."[2] At that time, Paul was talking about the difference between eating meat from the marketplace that may have been sacrificed to an idol and participating in the ceremonies at the idol's temple. This correlation seems to apply to Balaam. At first, God told him don't go and curse those people because they were blessed. The second time, God told Balaam he could go since Barak called for him again, but Balaam could only do what God instructed. The way Balaam left so quickly and without hesitation the next morning suggests that he was searching for a loophole to technically obey God but still have Barak's reward.[3]

What was really bizarre was that Balaam didn't even realize what he was doing. This is highlighted by the episode on the road with his donkey. Three times the poor beast saw God's angel and tried to save Balaam, only to be rewarded by a sever beating each time. The last time, God allowed the donkey to speak and show that she was more insightful than the prophet. As the scripture states, it was then that God "opened Balaam's eyes" and he saw the angel.[4] Once Balaam explicitly saw what he should have known, he became submissive and offered to return home. Once again, God said go but "speak only what I tell you."[5] That was the first of several parallels in this passage. Just as Balak called Balaam twice to come and curse Israel, with the second request having more prestigious ambassadors and promises of greater reward. God twice granted permission with the caveat of "speak only what I tell you," and the second time with a sterner warning.

Once Balaam reaches Moab, another set of parallels come about. Just as the angel stood in his way three times to kill him, Balaam blessed Israel three times when he was called to curse them.[6] This foreshadows Cephas (Peter) denying the Messiah three times[7] and then given, and taking, the chance to profess his love for his Lord three times.[8] (Isn't it amazing how many times three comes up when dealing with God?)

The next parallel can be seen in the curses turned to blessings if you look at them carefully. The first one Balaam says he "sees a people who live apart and do not consider themselves one of the nations. Who can count the dust of Jacob or number the fourth part of Israel?"[9] This blessing shows that God's first promise to Abraham has come to pass. His seed is now a great nation set apart from all the other nations of the world.

In his second blessing, Balaam speaks of God bringing Israel out of Egypt and "it will now be said … 'See what God has done!' The people rise like a lioness; they rouse themselves like a lion that does not rest till he devours his prey and drinks the blood of his victims."[10] This blessing shows that God's second promise to Abraham is about to come, and nothing can stop Israel from taking the land. This promise was emphasized at the beginning of the blessing when Balaam asked rhetorically about God, "Does He speak and then not act? Does He promise and not fulfill?"[11]

Balaam's third blessing is interesting in many ways. First of all, he says he sees the vision as "one whose eyes are opened."[12] The statement is interesting because at first he was too blind to see the angel his donkey saw. Balaam then goes on to say that Israel spreads out like a garden beside a river, water will flow from buckets, and "their seed" will have abundant water—as in giving "living water."[13] He adds that their king will be greater than any king of legend, and their kingdom will be exalted. In this blessing, Balaam is pointing to the one promise yet to be fulfilled. To emphasize it, Balaam restates at the end part of the second blessing about God bringing Israel out of Egypt and the people being like a lion ready to strike.

These blessings parallel God's covenant so completely as to be a return to the theme of Abraham. Balaam's final part of the blessings highlights this theme when he gives the same blessing God gave to Abraham, "May those who bless you be blessed and those who curse you be cursed."[14]

And here is a theme that is hinted at as it is repeated throughout the Bible—the curse turned into a blessing. We see this theme with Joseph's brothers meaning him harm but God allowing his slavery to turn to nobility that saves his family. Then Job is tormented, but his ordeal binds him closer to God. Samson is betrayed and blinded, and yet his greatest triumph comes out of this degradation.[15] And it is only after the Messiah suffers His accursed death of hanging on a tree that the victorious blessing of resurrection and redemption occur. Over and over again, what the world would see as a curse is really the beginning of a blessing. Can it be a coincidence that Jewish culture sees the start of new day at the setting of the sun? For the unbelieving world, the greatest tragedy is to die, and the greatest evil is to kill. But Christians must remember Paul's words, "to die is gain."[16]

Paul or Jonah

Had Balaam stayed home after returning from Peor, his name would not be a byword for a corrupting a teacher. Instead, he chose to give Balak, and the Midianites, some very evil counsel. When Balak first saw Israel, and what they did against the Amorites, he knew the Moabites couldn't win a pitch battle. And Balaam showed they could not be cursed. So Balak took the third option advocated by Balaam, corrupt the Israelites. Because of Balaam, the Midianites entered the camp and seduced the people to worship Ba'al of Peor. In the end, his guidance resulted in more than 24,000 Israelites dying of plague, the Midianite cities being destroyed, his own death, and his name becoming infamous. He is synonymous for one who forsakes the holiness God offers for the false glory of the world and who drags others down with him.

His final destruction is in sharp contrast to the recurring themes and dilemmas of the Bible—God's power and design verses humanity's free will. It first comes up with God hardening Pharaoh's heart to serve His purpose and then with Jonah being forced to go to Nineveh. Later in the New Testament, we have verses speaking of our preordainment and even Saul of Tarsus (Paul) being selected from the womb to be God's apostle to the gentiles. But we also see Joshua choosing to follow God, and Job selecting not to curse God. At humanity's very start, God gave us the power to choose when He told Cain to overcome the sin that crouched at the door for him. God always gave man freewill, but it is freewill within the confines of His design.

Balaam shows best how this freewill works. God allowed him to go to Moab, but only to say what God told him to say. Here, Balaam could not oppose God any more than he could prevent the sun from rising in the east. But he did have the freewill to try corrupting Israel. In like fashion, Jonah could not resist God in going to Nineveh, but he had the freewill to go kicking and screaming the whole time and to hope for the city's destruction. Paul on the other hand freely embraced God's ordainment and was the evangelist to kings, rulers, and gentiles. Our will cannot contest God's destiny for us, but we are free to be either a Jonah or a Paul.

Chapter 22 Endnotes

[1] Numbers 22:12 and 20.
[2] I Corinthians 10:23 (New American Standard).
[3] Numbers 22:21.
[4] Numbers 22:31.
[5] Numbers 22:35.
[6] Numbers 23-24.
[7] Matthew 26; Mark 14; Luke 22; and John 18.
[8] John 21:15–17.
[9] Numbers 23:9–10.
[10] Numbers 23:23–24.
[11] Numbers 23:19.
[12] Numbers 24:3 (King James)
[13] Numbers 24:7.
[14] Numbers 24:9.
[15] Judges 16.
[16] Philippians 1:21.

23

It is Finished

At the Sermon on the Mount, Christ made the statement that He had come not to abolish the Torah but to fulfill it, or complete it.[1] This statement implies that the Torah was incomplete. But how could it be deficient? Are there any situations or details of life it fails to touch on? Or is there something lacking on the fundamental level?

Do you remember Jesus' response to the scribes' question of what is the greatest commandment? Without hesitation, Christ said, "Love the Lord your God with all your heart, your soul, your mind and your strength This is the first and greatest commandment. And the second is like it: 'Love your neighbor as yourself.' All the Law and all the Prophets hang on these two commandments."[2] With those two commandments, how could the Torah be wanting? What more is needed?

If we think of the Bible as one continuous composition, then certain themes introduced first in the Torah should be revisited in the Gospels. And those things have appeared. The bread and wine with Melchizedek and Joseph are seen again in the Last Supper. The sins of the Israelites in the wilderness correspond to Christ's temptations. The life stories of Joseph and Moses are played again the life of Christ—and more and more can be added.

So let's look at another theme that is repeated in the Torah and replayed again in the Gospel. It is the going down into Egypt and being called out from Egypt. This first happens with Abraham,[3] then with Moses[4] (true, he started in Egypt, but after the burning bush, he went down and came back out), and happens again with Jesus.[5] Each man is unique, and each one marshals in a separate age: with Abraham the patriarchs, with Moses the Law, and with Jesus the Messianic age. But more than that, each man is the personification of an aspect of the Torah making it complete.

Reflect on Abraham's defining moment—the sacrifice of Isaac. Here was the child of promise that Abraham had waited almost all of his life. The child named for laughter who brought ultimate joy and hope into Abraham's old age, and who Abraham loved more than even his own life, maybe more than anything. He was to sacrifice this child, and he did it willingly. Only God's intercession saved Isaac's life. But in this whole affair, Abraham showed that his love of God was the greatest of all. He loved God with ever fiber of his being; he loved Him with all his heart, strength, soul, and mind.

With Moses, we see how to love your neighbor as yourself. He showed this by giving the law. Many misinterpret the law as being ruthless with its exact punishments and numerous capital punishments. But it was actually quite benevolent. It demanded justice for all—the weak and the strong.[6] It assured the survival of the poorest of the community by setting aside the corners of the fields for them to glean.[7] It prohibited ill-proportioned punishment by requiring an eye for an eye and a tooth for a tooth, rather than a heart for an eye or a head for a tooth.[8] Most important, the law was to be applied to everyone equally. The foreigner and the slave had the Sabbath rest and the same justice.[9] In short, it went into excruciating detail to ensure that, in every conceivable aspect, the Israelites treated one another exactly how they would want to be treated. In other words, it made sure that, through their actions, they loved their neighbor as themselves.

Not only the Torah, but through his life, Moses displayed the concept of loving your neighbor. Out of love for his people, he chose to accept the life of a slave.[10] He returned to Egypt to free the Israelites. Even though it was the last thing in the world he wanted to do, he still went. And no matter how the people tested, challenged, and exasperated him, he still shepherded them and pleaded for them before God. He loved them as he loved himself.

Looking at Abraham and Moses, we see how the two greatest commandments were shown in their lives. So by looking at Jesus' life, we may see what could be the final pillar that holds the completed Torah. Think back on the commandments that Jesus gave to His disciples. In all the searching of the Gospels, He gave only three commandments. At the Last Supper, He said, "do this in remembrance of me";[11] at His ascension, He gave the Great Commission by saying, "go and make disciples of all nations, baptizing them";[12] and in the garden, He told them, "Love one another. As I have loved you, ... Greater love has no one than this, that He lay down his life for his friends."[13] His life, and His death, were that last commandment personified. His final words on the cross were, "It is finished!" Another way to say it, "Now, it is complete." His willingness to die for His friends and for an evil world showed the greatest love of all. We can say that it is on this commandment hangs all the Gospel and all the Epistles.

Now we have the completed Torah with its bedrock commandments that are eternal and unchangeable. The first is to love the Lord your God with all your heart, with all your soul, with all your strength, and with all your mind. The second is like it: love your neighbor as yourself. And the third completes it: love your brother as Christ has loved you by laying down your life!

Why Egypt?

Why Egypt? Why not have Abram, Israel, and Jesus sent to another land? There has to be a reason, and Robert Alter gives us the rational explanation.[14] Alter shows the Bible's sense of irony when Jacob was grieving for Joseph and wailed, "Surely, I will go down to Sheol [grave or underworld] to my son mourning."[15] Instead, Jacob went down to Egypt to be with Joseph. Be aware that Egypt's religion was a death cult. On the west side of the Nile was where the city of the dead, with all its tombs, laid. Many claim the Egyptians were resurrectionists because of their opulent crypts and rite of mummification, but this idea is an error. Their tombs, with all the treasures, were seen as having spiritual elements that they would use in the land of the dead. The spells in their Book of the Dead were to guide them through their journey, not to resurrect them to a new life. In effect, Egypt was symbolic of the underworld (Sheol); for Abram, Moses, and Jesus to come up from Egypt was for them to be resurrected with new lives. Moreover, it shows that following their examples is the way to conquer death.

Chapter 23 Endnotes

[1] Matthew 5:17.
[2] Matthew 22:34–40 and Luke 10:27.
[3] Genesis 12:10.
[4] Exodus 4:17–19.
[5] Matthew 2:13–19.
[6] Leviticus 19:5; Deuteronomy 24:17 and 27:19.
[7] Leviticus 23:22.
[8] Leviticus 24:20.
[9] Exodus 12:49 and 20:10.
[10] Hebrews 11:24-25
[11] Luke 22:19.
[12] Matthew 28:19.
[13] John 13:34 and 15:13.
[14] Robert Alter, *The Art of Biblical Narrative* (New York: Basic Books, 1981), p. 4.
[15] Genesis 37:35 (American Standard Version).

Bibliography

Alter, Robert, *The Art of Biblical Narrative* (New York: Basic Books, 1981).

Cahill, Thomas, *The Gift of the Jews: How a Tribe of Nomads Changed the Way Everyone Thinks and Feels* (New York: Doubleday, 1998).

Dart, John. "Scriptural Schemes: The ABCBAs of Biblical Writing," *Christian Century*, July 13, 2004.

Dostoevsky, Fyodor, *The Brothers Karamazov* (Lyndhurst, NJ: Barnes and Noble Classics, 1994).

Frankl, Victor E., *Man's Search for Meaning*, (New York: Pocket Books, 1971, original 1959).

Gudder, Stanley, *A Mathematical Journey* (New York: McGraw-Hill Inc., 1976).

Jacobs, A. J., *The Year of Living Biblically: One Man's Humble Quest to Follow the Bible as Literally as Possible* (New York: Simon & Schuster, 2007).

Josephus, Flavius, *Antiquitates Judaicae*, book 14, chapter 4.

Kaplan, Aryeh, *The Handbook of Jewish Thought, Volume 2* (New York: Moznaim Publishing Corp., 1992).

Lewis, C. S. *The Abolition of Man* (New York: Simon & Schuster, 1944), appendix, "Illustrations of the Toa."

Morris, Desmond, *Babywatching* (New York: Crown Publishing, 1992).

Rosen, Ceil, and Moishe Rosen, *Christ in the Passover: Why Is This Night Different?* (Chicago, IL: Moody Press, 1978).

Schultz, Samuel J., *The Old Testament Speaks*, 2nd edition (New York: Harper & Row Publishers, 1960, 1970)

Sitchin, Zecharia, *Genesis Revisited: Is Modern Science Catching Up with Ancient Knowledge?* (Rochester: VT: Bear and Company, 1991).

Wilkinson, Richard H., *The Complete Gods and Goddesses of Ancient Egypt*, (London: Thames & Hudson, 2003)

PBS Religion and Ethics, "Torah Restoration," Episode 247, July 23, 1999.

The Holy Bible, American Standard Version, King James Version, New International Version, New American Standard Version.

Other Readings

Keller, Werner. *The Bible as History*, 2nd revised edition (Lyndhurst, NJ: Barnes and Noble Books, 1980).
Rohl, David M., *Pharaohs and Kings: A Biblical Quest* (New York: Crown Publishing, 1995).
Strobel, Lee, *The Case for Faith* (Grand, MI: Zondervan, 2000).

CPSIA information can be obtained at www.ICGtesting.com
Printed in the USA
BVOW071542080812

297354BV00003B/343/P